A Washington Sketchbook

Drawings by ROBERT L. DICKINSON, 1917–1918

A Washington Sketchbook

Drawings by ROBERT L. DICKINSON, 1917–1918

GAIL DICKERSIN SPILSBURY

Chesapeake
BOOK COMPANY

© 2011 Gail Dickersin Spilsbury

Designed by Denise Arnot

 The C&O Canal Trust made publication of this book possible. Founded in 2007, the C&O Canal Trust is the official nonprofit partner of the Chesapeake & Ohio Canal National Historical Park. Its mission is to work in partnership with the National Park Service to protect, restore, and promote the C&O Canal. The Trust engages communities and individuals to realize the Park's historical, natural, and recreational potential. For more information regarding the Trust, please visit www.canaltrust.org.

The *Washington Star* banner above Rambler quotations in this book was adapted to suggest the look of the original columns. © *Washington Post*; reprinted by permission of the DC Public Library.

Robert Shosteck's maps reproduced in this volume can be found in the Wanderbirds Vertical File, Washingtoniana Division, Martin Luther King Jr. Library, Washington, DC. Research suggests that they probably came from the back pocket of Robert Shosteck's *Guide to Trails around Washington,* © Robert Shosteck, 1937. This shortened citation is used in the book.

Unless otherwise noted, the drawings in this book are from Robert L. Dickinson's "A Washington Walk Book," the artist's notebook of original sketches housed in the Prints and Photographs Division, Library of Congress.

Cover image: Prospect Rock, detail, p. 49. Digital transfer and color correction by Ernie Brooks, Rock Creek Images. *Title page:* Franklin Park, detail, p. 100; *Endnotes:* St. John's Church, detail, p. 106; *Endpaper:* Dickinson's map, detail; *Back jacket flap:* Author photo: Ernie Brooks, Rock Creek Images.

Scans and color correction by DodgeChrome, www.dodgechrome.com.

ISBN: 978-0-9823049-3-8 (alk. paper)

Printed in China

Library of Congress Cataloging-in-Publication Data

Dickinson, Robert Latou, 1861–1950.
A Washington Sketchbook: Drawings by Robert L. Dickinson, 1917–1918 / Gail Dickersin Spilsbury.

p. cm.

"The drawings in this book are from Robert L. Dickinson's "A Washington Walk Book," the artist's notebook of original sketches, Prints and Photographs Division, Library of Congress.

Includes bibliographical references.

1. Dickinson, Robert Latou, 1861–1950, artist. Washington walkbook. 2. Washington (D.C.)—Description and travel. 3. Washington (D.C.)—Pictorial works. 4. Washington (D.C.)—History. 5. Washington Region—Description and travel. 6. Washington Region—Pictorial works. 7. Washington Region—History. 8. Potomac River—Description and travel. 9. Potomac River—Pictorial works. 10. Historic sites—Washington (D.C.) 11. Historic sites—Washington (D.C.)—Pictorial works. I. Spilsbury, Gail Dickersin. II. Dickinson, Robert Latou, 1861–1950. Washington walkbook. III. Title.

F195.D53 2011

975.3—dc23

2011018890

Contributors

A Washington Sketchbook has come to print through the generous support of the following individuals, organizations, foundations, and businesses:

Hugh Barbour

Ian Barbour

The Albert and Lillian Small Foundation

Furthermore: a program of the J. M. Kaplan Fund

The Max and Victoria Dreyfus Foundation

The Kiplinger Foundation

The Association of the Oldest Inhabitants

James F. Olmsted

The Lois and Richard England Family Foundation

The Eagle Family

Margaret Irwin Miller

Cabin John Citizens Association

Deecy Gray

Dick Jorgensen

Cleveland Park Historical Society

To GRD *&* BBD

Contents

I n the fall of 1917, a distinguished New York obstetrician and gynecologist named Robert Latou Dickinson (1861–1950) came to Washington, DC, to serve on the Army's General Medical Board as part of the nation's war effort. Dickinson brought with him another talent—art—and a passion for nature. In his free time he explored the Potomac River, sketching its beauty from Great Falls to the popular recreational sites on its Maryland and Virginia shores. He was already involved in illustrating the *New York Walk Book*, which is still in print today. As his Washington excursions grew, he planned a similar "walk book" for the nation's capital and made sketches for it. Before he could compile the volume, the war ended, and Dickinson returned to his medical career in New York, which included leadership in founding Planned Parenthood with Margaret Sanger.

Several years before his death at age eighty-nine, Dickinson donated his three-ring binder of Washington sketches to the Library of Congress, where the drawings sat undisturbed for sixty years. During the research phase for this book, Dickinson's grandsons, Hugh and Ian Barbour, produced their grandfather's hand-drawn, cultural-history map of the Potomac. This extraordinary map, annotated in the artist's own hand, identifies the places he visited and sketched. The map also captures a way of life along the Potomac during a different era, now lost to today's fast-paced commercial metropolis. Dickinson's legacy, through his map and drawings, recovers a segment of forgotten history in an original way. His charmingly rendered images inspire us to respect nature and find joy in experiencing the outdoors; they also remind us to treasure and preserve Washington's parks and historic landmarks.

A Washington Sketchbook presents Dickinson's Washington oeuvre with historic annotations about the places. While creating his walk book sketches, Dickinson made the acquaintance of two local nature aficionados—"the Rambler," who wrote excursion pieces for the *Evening Star* in the early twentieth century, and Robert Shosteck, who contributed hiking expeditions to the *Washington Post* in the 1930s. Shosteck's Sunday hikes encouraged Washingtonians to explore their environs and led to founding the enduring Wanderbirds hiking club and the 1935 *Potomac Trail Book*. We know from old photographs that the Rambler accompanied

Dickinson to Prospect Rock, one of the Potomac's most dramatic physical features and shown on the cover of this book.

Finding out about Dickinson—the fascinating man behind the drawings—led to my reading his personal papers at Harvard University's Countway Medical Library. Without question Dickinson's life deserves a full-length biography; his medical research alone, on women's sexuality and marriage, was pioneering. I have prepared for this volume a brief biographical sketch highlighting his major achievements. The section covering his Washington years (1917–1918) begins on page 166.

Every book is a journey of the people behind it, and so many people contributed in small and large ways to this book. I am grateful to them all. Hugh Barbour, Dickinson's grandson, consistently provided enthusiasm and generous support for the project, as did his brother Ian. The Association of the Oldest Inhabitants of the District of Columbia gave a grant to support the reproduction of Dickinson's original drawings in the Library of Congress. Early on the Tenleytown Historical Society's fiscal sponsorship of the research allowed the project to move forward. The C&O Canal Trust's subsequent sponsorship has seen the book through to publication. I am particularly grateful to Matt Logan who recognized the value of Dickinson's drawings in relation to the preservation of Washington's unmatched Potomac landscape and other historic sites. Furthermore: a program of the J. M. Kaplan Fund, generously supported the book's design. The Albert and Lillian Small Foundation gave a significant boost to the fundraising drive, and the Lois and Richard England Family Foundation saw the educational merit in the book and contributed support. Deep appreciation to the Kiplinger Foundation for giving the project another push forward. It was an honor to gain the help of individuals and organizations located along the Potomac and dedicated to its integrity, including the Eagle Family, Cabin John Citizens Association, and Deecy Gray. Other grants followed making publication possible.

The Library of Congress Publications Office generously provided copyediting of the manuscript thanks to Ralph Eubank's early support of the project. Ernie Brooks, nature photographer extraordinaire, contributed photographs and handled many time-consuming reproduction issues. Joe Spilsbury answered every call for emergency assistance with a cheerful, "Of course." His brother Bob pitched in with the final proofreading of layouts. Ulrike Mills did an excellent job as principal proofreader. Librarians, cartographers, historians, associations, outdoor clubs, and local residents all spent time with me, discussing my research, and providing advice and expertise, particularly in areas where no official records could be found. Some questions remain unanswered, but just as many led to new nuggets of information. Special thanks go to Peggy Appleman, Peter DeVincentis, Tabitha Eagle, Joe Hage, Faye Haskins, Drew Kleibrink, Adam Lewis, Norman Metzger, Carol Niedzialek, Jim Olmsted, James Perry, Dave Pierce, Gail Redman, Ryan Shepard, Scott Southworth, Perry Wheelock, and the Historical Society of Washington, DC. Many experts on Washington, Maryland, and Virginia history reviewed the manuscript and offered valuable suggestions. Others provided willing assistance and advice. I wish to thank all these individuals: Tanya Beauchamp, Chris Black, Richard Cook, Steve Dryden, John Fox, Pamela Henson, Mike High, Lynn Hutcheson, Howard Kaplan, Jerry McCoy, Ross Netherton, Jo-Ann Neuhaus, Wally Owen, Peter Penczer, Rod Sauter, and Mary Thompson. The patient staff at Fedex Kinkos, Government Center, Boston, churned out countless layouts and other jobs for the book and deserve thanks. Denise Arnot's imaginative design highlights Dickinson's artwork in a way that would delight him. I am grateful to Ric Cottom, my publisher, who said yes to this project, handled it with flexibility, and offered valuable advice at every stage of the production process.

Readers should note that misspellings or style irregularities in the quoted Rambler articles from the *Evening Star* follow the original columns. Other early twentieth-century spelling anomalies have been retained, such as "bowlder." A few typographical errors in source material have been corrected to help the reader. In the captions to Dickinson's drawings, some upper- and lower- case letters have been altered for consistent presentation.

GDS
Washington, DC, 2011

The Call of the Outdoors

Again the witching season has come when nature uses every wile to lure the lover of the outdoors to desert the army that throngs the city pavements and slip away to discover anew the charms of quiet woodland paths, of wandering brooks, of cool, clear lakes, of wave-washed beaches, or of sweeping views from mountain heights. What riches nature has to offer all who will but pause to behold. And even the richest in worldly possessions is poor in spirit if there is nothing in him that rises in wonder and admiration at the changing panorama of the seasons—spring's delicate mantle of green, embroidered with flowers and jeweled with glistening raindrops; verdant meadows spread under the blue of midsummer skies; gorgeous-hued autumn, whose brief glory fades into quiet grays and somber browns; the majesty of trees in winter. There is no break in the miraculous cycle, and any day is a good day to enjoy its marvels. —Editor, *Bulletin,* Potomac Appalachian Trail Club, April 1932

Great Falls and the
C&O Canal

Great Falls and the C&O Canal

Every visitor to the Potomac River's Great Falls experiences the same thrilling sensation. Water surges over jagged rocks between wild riverbanks; nature is at her most powerful, her most striking. A feeling of awe and reverence instantly rises up, along with an urge to be part of the landscape. For centuries, recreation along the Potomac has been as constant as quiet appreciation of its bucolic beauty.

Long before European settlers came to these shores, native tribes inhabited the area. Yet for Americans, the river's history begins much later, with the life and leadership of one of their favorite presidents, George Washington. As a Virginian, Washington grew up and pursued early surveying and military experiences near the Potomac. His home, Mount Vernon, was located on the Potomac. Throughout his life, this was his river, his land, his deepest passion, although he always put the welfare of the new country ahead of his land-development pursuits. It is not surprising that Washington's love for the river contributed to creating the new nation's capital just below the famous falls. The country he had fought for and been elected to lead would have a permanent connection to the place most sacred in his heart. Washington, DC, is aptly named.

Although George Washington's early initiative to create a trade route to Ohio's western frontier by building a canal system to bypass Great Falls ultimately failed, it led to preserving for future Washingtonians one of the most pastoral and beautiful landscapes anywhere on earth—the Chesapeake and Ohio (C&O) Canal with its timeless towpath. For, more than a century after the canal project was abandoned, a New Deal initiative set a precedent for conserving this land along the river's District and Maryland shore stretching from Georgetown to Cumberland, Maryland, not far from the Potomac's source. The Virginia shore from Key Bridge to Great Falls stands in contrast to the canal side. Here, a thin Potomac Heritage Trail follows the shoreline below the drone of the George Washington Parkway, and beyond Chain Bridge, private development on the gorge's cliffs has ended the possibility of public hiking to such wonders as Prospect Rock (see page 48). Fortunately Great Falls Park, Virginia, preserves several miles of trails, inspiring lookouts, and the remnants of President Washington's Patowmack Canal Company, including stone foundations and a stone chimney from the Matildaville settlement created to support the enterprise.

Heaps of rocks are scattered about—enormous granite bowlders and jagged reefs of gneiss—as if some Titan of long ago had vented his wrath by upheaving the crust of the earth itself. The wildness of the place, as waters churn and boil in their never-ending warfare with the rocks, is comparable only to some of the larger mountain canyons of the West, and is hard to conceive as being within a few miles of the Capital City. —Gilbert Grosvenor, President, National Geographic Society, 1928

Then there's that other river, the rabid animal, flushed with red earth and swollen with snowmelt or frog-strangling rains. It leaps its banks, brutally sweeping all before it, leaving gouged fields and splintered forests. —Wilbur E. Garrett, *National Geographic,* 1987

TOSSING WATER · GREAT FALLS 1918

The River

Like so many Washingtonians who enjoy the scenic pleasures and birding opportunities of the Potomac River from Georgetown to Seneca, Robert Latou Dickinson made this stretch of river the focus of his drawings during his war service years, 1917–1918. The river's wild rock formations and dangerously frothing waters that suddenly change to meandering tranquility captured his imagination. A unique pictorial record resulted, documenting the river with its famous twists and turns, canal with locks, narrow gorge, swimming holes, and campsites. Few major cities offer such abundant recreational potential within minutes of work and home.

The Potomac's Mather Gorge rock is about six hundred million years old. Over this stretch of time, continental plate collisions caused the sedimentary and igneous rock to metamorphose into schist, gneiss, and migmatite, with quartz, white and black mica, garnet, staurolite, and kyanite forming as the rocks cooled. During this evolutionary process, the "downcutting" river has eroded the bedrock, causing the famous falls to recede upstream from their earlier position near Chain Bridge. Erosion has also changed the river's course. "Evidence of the ancient river beds can be seen in well-rounded boulders, smoothed surfaces and grooves, and beautifully formed potholes. ... The metamorphic rocks provide jagged rocky surfaces and high-walled cliffs, stark and pristine against the crashing waters of the Potomac at the falls and along Mather Gorge." The U.S. Geological Survey map of the Mather Gorge (page 188) shows the area's various rocks and their historic age. It also highlights the river's level surfaces known as terraces, which are the remains of old flood plains. Of these six discernible terraces, Glade Hill in Great Falls Park is the oldest and the highest. The downcutting Potomac also created "islands, islets, pinnacles, shoestring channels, oxbows, plunge pools, and potholes" in these terraces. For example, Widewater (see page 32) was an abandoned channel that the C&O Canal followed. The channel also partly creates Bear Island, where the river's erosional impact can be clearly seen.[1]

The Potomac's North Branch headwaters are found at the Fairfax Stone, West Virginia; its longer South Branch component feeds in at Potomac Forks, near Oldtown, Maryland. Both branches had earlier Indian names with various spellings.

For colonists in the 1600s, and for generations after, the river was a principal means of transportation and the region's commercial focal point. From the outset of settlement, John Smith and other explorers, including George Washington,

Tossing Water,
Great Falls, 1918.

sought a passage to the north and west via the river. Little Falls prevented Smith from further navigation, as he recorded:

> Having gone so high as we could with the bote, we met divers Salvages [*sic*] in Canowes, well loaden with the flesh of Beares, Deere, and other beasts, whereof we had part, here we found mighty Rocks, growing in some places above the grownd as high as the shrubby trees, and divers other solid quarries of divers tinctures; and divers places where the waters had falne from the high mountaines they had left a tinctured spangled skurfe, that made many bare places seeme as guilded. Digging the growne above in the highest clifts of rocks, we saw it was claie sand so mingled with the yeallow spangles as if it had beene halfe pin-dust.[2]

In 1748, George Washington's surveying apprenticeship for Lord Thomas Fairfax took him into the Appalachian Mountains. Five years later, at age twenty-one, he volunteered for a military mission to prevent the French from claiming the Forks of the Ohio, today's Pittsburgh. This territorial dispute led to the French and Indian War and to Washington's deepening interest in western trade routes along the Potomac. In the years after the frontier wars, Washington acquired more than 30,000 acres of land with access to the Potomac and began planning with fellow investors how to make the river more navigable. The War of Independence interrupted his efforts, but once it ended, his Virginia colleagues Thomas Jefferson and James Madison persuaded him to launch the Patowmack Company, which he then formed in 1785.[3]

Over the course of the seventeenth century, agrarian settlements spread along the lower Potomac. Pioneers generally were poor, but land was cheap and large tracts of 5,000 to 10,000 acres were commonly purchased in Maryland and Virginia. English settlers aspired to the lifestyle of the mother country's landed aristocracy and over time built mansions on plantations with miles of riverfront, which quickly came to depend on slave labor. Smaller land tracts went to early settlers who worked as artisans or servants. Land, not a bank account, was the measure of wealth. The region's enormous estates meant a dispersed population, so that the port towns of Alexandria, Georgetown, and Baltimore became trading hubs and centers of social life.[4]

On both sides of the Potomac, tobacco was the mainstay of the early economy, and the river carried it to port. "Rolling roads," especially in Virginia, led from barns to boat landings; huge tobacco containers rolled down these roads to the river, where ships took them to sea. In time, dozens of ferryboats—most propelled by sail or oar until 1813—crisscrossed the Potomac, and old maps show their names and "landings." White's Ferry (formerly Conrad's Ferry, begun in 1782), located above Harrison's Island, is the only one still operating today.[5]

The river and the cold have conspired to become co-creators of the most beautiful sculpture. The frozen river has become a canvas for the artistic whims of the freezing water. From above looking down, the river is a myriad of white shapes trapped under layers of textured and fissured glass. A closer look reveals the geometric precision of the ice crystals whose forms are as varied as the snowflake's, from miniature spires to intricate basket weaves with patterns both subtle and complex. It is a masterpiece unmatched and ever changing. —Joe Hage, Sycamore Island Club Caretaker, 2004

Great Falls of the Potomac in the big freeze for 1918, the green water spouting out beneath arches two feet in thickness

Great Falls of the Potomac in the Big Freeze of 1918; the green water spouting out beneath arches two feet in thickness.

Many ferrymen operated taverns and hostelries, and with the development of roads and stagecoach lines in the later 1700s, "ordinaries," or inns, dotted the land routes that followed the river.[6] Until the post–Civil War period, Washington was a rough-hewn town that lacked amenities and infrastructure, although local commerce bustled. Perhaps it resembled a western frontier town with similar freedom from municipal regulation. At the time of George Washington's Patowmack Canal Company in the late eighteenth century, U.S. currency was in short supply and Spanish, French, British, Portuguese, and even Arab specie was accepted for tolls. Barter was common and whiskey was a preferred trade item.[7] Frederick Tilp writes in his history of the river that its central role in the region even encompassed seduction. By 1840, offshore bathhouses transformed into nighttime brothels where, according to a local reporter, "attentive lads known as 'Billy-boys' will gladly row anxious gentlemen out to a bath house of their choice for joys with their bewitching Lorelei maidens."[8] Piney Point, known as the summer White House because various presidents from James Madison to Theodore Roosevelt summered there, reputedly had five such pavilions. Later, floating barges replaced the pavilion bathhouses as "approved houses of ill fame," and their heyday followed the Civil War as a result of "easy money on Washington's commercialized and crowded waterfront."[9] The "Potomac Ark" houseboats used by fishermen and shipyard workers gradually came into the hands of gamblers and their ilk who formed "ark colonies" in Washington Harbor. By the Gay Nineties, arks were "the perfect floating craft for illicit boy-girl operations, because of their mobility in deep or shoal waters, in the open river, or at the headwaters of swamps."[10] Attempted police raids failed because of the ark colony's ability to communicate warnings. Usually arks were one-woman enterprises, ranked according to the owner's reputation. Ark trafficking on the Virginia side began to decline in the late 1920s, during preparations for constructing the George Washington Parkway; in Maryland arks continued to thrive through World War II. According to Tilp, as late as 1976 several glamorous "sex-houseboats" owned by congressmen and lobbyists moored at the Columbia Island Marina. Arlington, too, had a seedier side in Rosslyn and Jackson City, the latter located at the end of Long Bridge, today's Fourteenth Street bridge. There, in the late nineteenth century, investors built gambling houses and soon "the Monte Carlo of Virginia" flourished.[11]

Certainly as you travel up the river away from the city's active waterfront, a different kind of scene prevails, one of astonishing natural beauty, and because of George Washington's focus on it, a territory rich in history and lore. Much of its unique tradition has roots in the Chesapeake and Ohio Canal, second only to the river as a beloved physical feature of the nation's capital.

C&O Canal

A sense of magic permeates the C&O Canal. Surrounded by trees, rocks, and sublime views, walkers and bikers traveling along the sandy towpath experience the enchantment captured in Dickinson's drawings. Part of the idyllic setting comes from the canal's unusual history. Its roots date back to President George Washington's Patowmack Canal Company in Great Falls, Virginia, where between the years 1785 and 1802 the company constructed five locks to circumvent the waterfalls and enable trade with the Ohio frontier and ultimately, lands farther west, up the river. These locks, which accommodated a seventy-seven-foot drop in the river, operated until 1830. Another three locks had to be built at the far end of the two-mile stretch of canal around Little Falls, to raise and lower boats thirty-eight feet (see page 29). At Seneca Falls, Virginia, the canal bypassed a mile of rapids with a seven-foot drop. In all, the Patowmack Company waterway carried some $10 million dollars' worth of goods from the Cumberland and Ohio region to Georgetown, but only one dividend of $5.55 was ever paid to its stockholders; the company ended in bankruptcy, its rights transferred to the C&O Company in 1828.[13]

Although the Patowmack and C&O Canal companies never profited, boat people moving the merchandise made a living for more than one hundred years and also left a legacy of canal life, which a New Deal initiative in the 1930s helped preserve. While boats and commerce operated, money was always in short supply, and workers to build or repair the canal were hard to find—"wages included three-quarters of a pint of rum every day."[14] A major obstacle to the canal's success was the river. Floods periodically devastated the canal, locks, and sluices, and droughts made the waterway impassable. But the factor most responsible for the canal's failure was the opening of the railroad. On the same day in July 1828 that President John Quincy Adams inaugurated the C&O Canal Company by digging a shovelful of earth near Georgetown, the Baltimore and Ohio Railroad (B&O) laid its cornerstone forty miles away, assisted by ninety-year-old Charles Carroll, the sole surviving signer of the Declaration of Independence.[15]

Even so, life along the canal between its inception in 1828 and decline in the 1880s (although it operated until 1924) filled the area with a spirit that lingers as nostalgia today. Washington—established in 1800 as the nation's capital—was a new and growing city, and commerce and recreation along the towpath carried a feeling of adventure. Cabin John, Glen Echo, Clara Barton's house, the Bobinger Hotel, Great Falls Tavern, locks and lockhouses, boats, camping, canoeing, fishing, and trade all contributed to the towpath's picturesque appeal.

The canal never reached the Ohio, stopping at Cumberland…but it did create a functioning flat-water route along the Potomac for 184.5 miles…with 74 locks, 11 aqueducts, scores of culverts, and a tunnel at Paw Paw that carries the canal 3,118 feet through a mountain. By the 1870s the C&O had spawned a boisterous trade involving 500 canal boats and 4,000 mules, mostly hauling coal.[12] —Joel Achenbach, author

The trip from Cumberland to Georgetown took from four to seven days, with boats carrying coal, lumber, building stone, and agricultural products; later the cargo was principally coal. The boatmen also carried liquor along with their personal provisions. The return trip brought fish, salt, fertilizer, iron ore, and manufactured goods to the frontier. During its peak year of 1875, the canal transported almost one million tons of goods.[16] Painted and decorated with flags, the boats were aptly named to reflect canal life: Darling, Rough and Ready, Cock Robin, Jenny Lind, Hero, Peacocks, Unexpected, American Flag, and the General George Washington. Canal boats averaged four miles per hour and made fewer than thirty trips per year. The C&O was not completed until 1850. Although it remained active for nearly seventy-five more years, its tonnage began to dwindle significantly after the 1870s. Excerpts from Frederick Doering's unpublished memoir capture the flavor of late-nineteenth-century life along the canal:

> We used to go back and fro to Georgetown [from Potomac, Maryland] by way of the Chesapeake and Ohio Canal. By road it took three and a half hours in summer and four hours in winter for a distance of seventeen miles. From Potomac to MacArthur [Conduit Road] in summer the dust was six inches deep and in winter eight to twelve inches of mud. When it was frozen the springless wagons were nearly shaken to pieces.
>
> There was seldom fresh meat in Potomac during the summer. John Stone a farmer in those days would butcher a cow or steer and share with his neighbors. There were a few icehouses and when the ice on the canal was thick enough they would cut it and haul it up from Sandy Landing Road. Mr. Stone gave up farming in the early nineties and bought the store from Mr. Winfield Offutt. In place of fresh beef most families raised chickens. The young lads would go to the river and catch cat-fish or tobacco-boxes [golden sun perch]. The two stores at Potomac sold salted, dried, and home cured smoked meat. The farmers in the area would salt or brine down large quantities of herring in 52-gallon vinegar barrels. They bought them from fellows at the Chain Bridge who dipped them from the river with a net and sold them for 10 cents a hundred. Marketing in Potomac was a casual operation before the 1900s. There was a Post Office in one of the two general merchandise stores. Ed Perry's store had a P.O. and therefore did the most business. They delivered on orders of $5.00 or more free. Considering the roads this was a real accommodation.[17]

River, towpath, canal, road and trolley. The vine covered cedar at the little station. Chain Bridge above Washington on the Potomac, Jan. 1918.

In Dickinson's day the trolley was part of the recreational spirit of the canal. Residents took trolleys and electric railways to towpath destinations for their day-long picnics or canoe adventures.

RIVER TOWPATH CANAL ROAD AND TROLLEY

The vine covered cedar at the little station

Chain Bridge above Washington on the Potomac, Ja. 1918.

The canal was the principal route to Georgetown for communities five or ten miles up the river. Georgetown was a bustling port city and trading post. Country people took their crops and cord wood to town and returned with food and farm supplies. According to Doering:

> There were two mule-drawn canal boats converted to carry passengers, instead of coal. They used to charter these on Sundays for parties from Georgetown to Great Falls. One way trip usually took five hours barring accidents. There was always great excitement on these trips from the time they left the dock to the four hours spent at Great Falls Hotel picnicking and walking on the swinging bridge over "Falls Branch" to return at night-fall and hurrying over the wharf, around Water's warehouse up to High Street and finally the old horse cars were in sight and safety![18]

Otho Swain, born on a canal boat in 1901 and interviewed by Elizabeth Kytle for a bicentennial Cabin John memory book, told of his grandfather's days building the canal's Paw Paw tunnel: "They were cutting through rock by hand with drills. This tunnel is a mile long under a mountain…. They didn't have any machinery to excavate with, just horses and mules and plows and scoops." Most canal workers were immigrants from Ireland, Germany, England, and the Netherlands. Work was torturous, wages were paltry, and on Saturday pay day workers would "get drunk and get to fighting and sometimes the National Guard would have to come to quiet them down." At one point, cholera struck and Swain's grandfather saw "forty men die in less than two hours"; they supposedly were buried on the hillside at Great Falls Tavern. "There's only one tombstone left; and all they said about him [was that] he was a stone cutter and he was twenty-five years old when he died; not even his name. When I was a child, there was a bunch of stones in there, but there's only one now."[19] Probably this history is laced with lore, as workers fled the canal area quickly when cholera struck in the 1830s. Also, the center of the outbreak was around Shepherdstown, and the National Park Service has identified the nameless stonecutter's grave as belonging to a Washington Aqueduct builder and not a canal laborer.[20]

Many of the locks' handsome stones came from the Seneca quarry (see page 73), and stonemasons were the most valued workmen on the canal. The Smithsonian Castle, the Renwick Gallery, and parts of Georgetown University and Cabin John Bridge are made of this beautiful red-brown stone.

Boats ran night and day, and while one mule team rested in the stable onboard, the other team pulled the boat along the towpath. "A canal boat was about 90 to 95 feet long, and about 14 and a half feet wide—only a few inches less wide than the locks," Swain recalled in his oral history. "The stable was in the front. In the middle was the hay house. At the back was what amounted to a little house on the boat— quarters for the captain and his wife and family. It had two bedrooms and a

Fifteen miles from Washington the Potomac gorge reaches its zenith in the Great Falls, where the river makes a majestic plunge over a series of granite terraces and a riotous profusion of giant boulders. —Albert W. Atwood, *National Geographic*, 1945

The Placid Canal and the Turbulent River;
the Potomac below Great Falls, 1918.

kitchen and a small dining room." Before her early death, Swain's mother cooked on the boat during the summer but stayed home in Sharpsburg the rest of the year, raising hogs and tending a garden. The men then took turns cooking in her absence. "In the morning you'd have cornbread, corn cakes. We'd make them the night before. And you'd have coffee and eggs and bacon. You ate a lot of ham, and lots of times you'd have fish. Fish that you'd catch yourself off the boat...big mouth bass and black bass—out of the canal and river.... Getting food along the canal was no problem. Most every 25 miles there'd be a grocery store.... Most of the stores were right at the locks."[21]

When Swain was about nine his father became a locktender, and Swain descendants continue to operate a concession at Swain's Lock, number 21, mile 16.7. The lockhouses from Georgetown to Monocacy Aqueduct (mile 24) are built of stone and resemble each other; they are thought to typify a vernacular architecture of the Upper Potomac Valley.[22]

Otho Swain became a boatman and never tired of river life with its daily parade of bear, eagles, goats, deer, reptiles, fish, and flowers. Between ten-day runs from Cumberland to Georgetown and back, he farmed, for boating pay never provided sufficient income. In 1919, he made his last trip, having decided he could earn a better living working at golf courses. For many years he tended the Burning Tree Club in Bethesda, Maryland, and in time built Dwight D. Eisenhower's White House putting green.[23]

After most of the canal closed in 1924, a unique lifestyle that had been fading since the late 1800s became obsolete and by the end of the Second World War left few traces. Walking the towpath today is like visiting a living museum, but only if you know something about the C&O Canal. Otherwise, it is simply beautiful parkland. As historian Mike High has written in his detailed study of the canal:

> While the decline of manufacturing and transportation has had a terrible effect on the valley towns, it has also restored the river to a more natural state. Following the canal towpath on foot or on a bicycle, it's hard to regret anything. Just a few miles north of Washington, the Potomac quickly becomes very quiet. The early visions of mills and furnaces and a water route teeming with boats on their way to the Ohio Valley never materialized, but the ebbing of industry has left a natural treasure.[24]

A number of factors led to the C&O Canal's failure, particularly its lack of revenue. Competition with the coal-carrying railroad and a series of floods eventually ground business to a halt. A flood in 1886, followed by another one in 1889 that "ripped down the Potomac Valley, bringing canal boats, lockhouses, and sheds tumbling into the river," resulted in bankruptcy.[25] The company's rival of many decades, the B&O Railroad, which had become the canal company's principal bondholder following its two previous mortgages in 1844 and 1878, stepped in to negotiate loans for the canal's repair. The Maryland court, a trustee of the C&O, agreed to the B&O's receivership, as long as it consented to continue canal operations. The Chesapeake and Ohio Transportation Company formed to replace the C&O, and in 1902 it became the Canal Towage Company, under which boats were given numbers and ran on a schedule. "[A]n era of individualism had come to an end: boat captains became company employees and were no longer the masters of their ships."[26] Low-volume traffic continued but only for the purpose of showing that the canal did business, in order to prevent sale to a competitor. After the 1924 flood brought canal commerce to a halt, the B&O made repairs from Lock 5 to Georgetown (five miles), where it could prove to the court that business still flourished by providing water power to several Georgetown mills. "[T]he B&O had no desire to return the obsolete, unprofitable canal to operation. Its primary concern was that the potentially valuable right-of-way not fall into the hands of a competitor, such as the Western Maryland Railway. If the property could be sold with assurance that it would not be used for commercial transportation, the railroad would be delighted."[27]

The Three Locks Close Together, nos. 12, 13, and 14, near Stubblefield Falls, 1918.

Today, Interstate 495, the Capital Beltway, cuts an ugly swath over the canal, concealing well-preserved Lock 13. People strolling the towpath in this vicinity will find an original stone mile marker at Lock 11, which reads: 9 miles to W. C. [Washington City]. Photo © 2004 Ernie Brooks, Rock Creek Images.

The Three Locks
close together
S= 1918

Nos. 12, 13, 14

The McMillan Commission's 1902 plan for Washington's beautification included an idea for preserving the picturesque riverfront through acquisition of the canal as National Park land, after which a "Potomac Drive" would be built along it. The commission's report stated that "The beauty of the scenery along the route of this proposed noble river-side improvement is so rare and, in the minds of the Commission, of so great value not only to Washingtonians, but to all visitors…that it should be safeguarded in every way."[28] The Depression helped the C&O's preservation because President Franklin D. Roosevelt liked the idea of purchasing the land in order to create jobs for the Civilian Conservation Corps (CCC). Intricate negotiations with the courts and the B&O followed, and in 1938 the government purchased most of the land for $2 million dollars. Although the Park Service administered the CCC's canal repairs from Georgetown to Seneca, the canal property was "not officially a unit of the national park system."[29] Those enrolled in CCC's Federal Project 712 were African Americans, and in just three years, they repaired twenty-three locks, the towpath, dikes, and some lockhouses. They constructed stone retaining walls and dams, water and sewer systems, parking lots for picnic areas, and concessions at Great Falls. The results were so successful that the National Park Service advocated complete restoration of the canal:

> It has been stated that nothing in or near Washington can compare in potential outdoor nature educational opportunities with the canal as a whole.… Stopping the geologic, biologic, and historic stories at Seneca is comparable to an arbitrary conclusion of a textbook at the end of the first few chapters. The upper regions of the canal penetrate life zones and geologic formations which are needed for the complete understanding of the area traversed between portions below Seneca.[30]

World War II put an end to canal restoration, and after the war the Army Corps of Engineers presented its plan for fourteen dams on the Potomac that would control floods and submerge the C&O Canal. Simultaneously a plan circulated for a scenic drive along the riverfront. When the *Washington Post* endorsed this plan in 1954, Supreme Court Justice William O. Douglas, a passionate environmentalist, wrote a letter to the editors, partially quoted below, inviting them to walk the entire towpath with him to witness its unparalleled beauty:

> The stretch of 185 miles of country from Washington, DC, to Cumberland, Md., is one of the most fascinating and picturesque in the Nation. The river and its islands are part of the charm. The

cliffs, the streams, the draws, the benches and beaches, the swamps are another part. The birds and game, and blaze of color in the spring and fall, the cattails in the swamp, the blush of buds in late winter— these are also some of the glory of the place.… It is a refuge, a place of retreat, a long stretch of quiet and peace at the Capital's back door— a wilderness area where we can commune with God and with nature, a place not yet marred by the roar of wheels and the sound of horns.[31]

The famous hike by Justice Douglas and canal supporters in March 1954 marked the turning point for making the C&O Canal a National Historical Park; however, it would take sixteen more years to pass the necessary legislation, as lobbyists for both the dam and the parkway proposals redoubled their efforts and even succeeded briefly with the razing of Lock 5 for the Clara Barton Parkway. Since 1971, the National Park Service has had to manage the serious floods of 1972 and 1985, along with its regular maintenance work. As Mike High notes in his *C&O Canal Companion*, continued Park Service efforts might ultimately result in the realization of President Washington's dreamed-of Potomac route to the west, even if today's purpose has become recreational rather than commercial:

In the end, the C&O Canal may finally outshine its rivals if the connection to the Ohio Valley is made by continuing the trail along the abandoned Western Maryland Railroad through the mountains. Part of this trail already exists…[and further extensions] will make it possible for hikers and bicyclists to travel all the way from Georgetown to Pittsburgh, crossing the Appalachians on a gently graded trail. Considering that much of the Erie Canal's towpath has disappeared along with its mules, the tables have suddenly turned. The C&O Canal may well become the only off-road trail to the west—an unexpected vindication of Jefferson and Washington's faith in the Potomac route.[32]

Widewater, C&O Canal,
near Washington.

Widewater is one of the most popular strolling areas of the towpath. Originally it was a channel in the Potomac that workers adapted into a segment of the canal. It spreads like a peaceful lake protected by woods and affords lovely reflections in the water and superb views of the river. Dickinson captured its romantic, timeless ambiance.

Widewater, C&O Canal,
below Great Falls, 1918.

Lock Tavern, Great Falls

Similar in style to other lockhouses along the lower Potomac, Great Falls Tavern (also called Lock Tavern or Crommelin House) stood at the hub of canal activity and today serves as the National Park Service's Visitor Center and museum. Built between 1828 and 1831 for the lockkeeper W. W. Fenlon, who supervised all six locks close to Great Falls, the Crommelin House (named for a Dutch investor in the canal) was to be a hotel for travelers as well as the lockkeeper's home. It quickly became the nucleus of the local community, a vibrant gathering place for holidays or rendezvous with friends. Nearly twenty years later, the Canal Company prohibited the sale of alcohol at the tavern, and a year later, in 1849, ruled that the building should serve only as a lockhouse, actions probably intended to tone down its role as a local tavern. In 1851 the north wing "Ball Room" became a grocery store, and in 1858 lockkeeper Henry Busey was permitted to reopen an ordinary (inn), to lodge guests. In the same period construction of the Washington Aqueduct (see page 81) damaged the building and also brought workers to the area. Later on, one of the aqueduct's former barracks located near today's traffic circle gained a second life by becoming a hotel, operated by Richard Jackson from the end of the Civil War to 1878. Described as a "slouchy, shiftless, greasy-haired man, whose humor is chiefly an appalling exhibit of his manifold offenses," Jackson attracted a rowdy clientele, for his establishment was just beyond the canal's "dry" boundaries.

During one of its incarnations, the lockhouse was also a club, and Dickinson's drawings suggest that this was its role in 1918, under the name Lock Tavern Club.[33]

Lock Tavern Club, Great Falls, Washington, DC.

Lock Tavern Club, Great Falls,
Washington, DC.

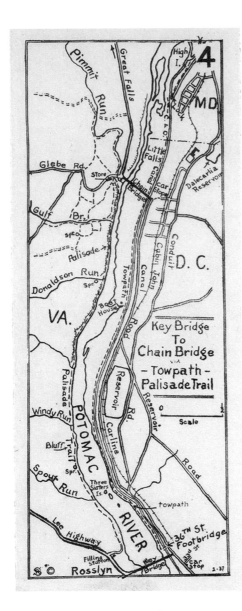

Key Bridge to Chain Bridge.
Robert Shosteck, *Guide to Trails around Washington.*
© Robert Shosteck, 1937.

Virginia's Potomac Shore

The C&O Canal characterizes one side of the Potomac River. The lush landscape of the Virginia side, where palisades drop precipitously to the water, also appears in Dickinson's Washington oeuvre. The artist hiked and sketched those rocks and shorelines on numerous occasions, and hikers could follow most of his tracks today if it weren't for private property preventing access.

Robert Shosteck (1910–1979), Hiking Leader and Preservationist

A number of hiking clubs existed in the Washington area before Robert Shosteck's inspiring treks in the mid-to-late 1930s, but it was his articles in the *Washington Post* and his leadership on weekly hikes along the Potomac River that galvanized the public into an unprecedented enthusiasm for exploring Washington's wilderness. Shosteck's weekly hikes with the Wanderbirds club he had formed led to his production of trail maps that soon came out in the classic *Potomac Trail Book* of 1935. Subsequent editions followed along with other tour books, all available in the Library of Congress; booksellers still have a supply of his *Potomac Trail Book*. In the later 1930s Shosteck started a second Capital City hiking club, and both it and the Wanderbirds continue to operate today.

Shosteck was the spark behind a huge surge in outdoor activities in both the District of Columbia and its surrounding counties. Yet, today's avid hikers have rarely heard of Shosteck or his pioneering trail books. Not only was his leadership important, but his maps and notes on hikes also provide a rare record of early trails, particularly on the Virginia side of the river, where private land development has ended public access. Dickinson hiked many of the same trails found in Shosteck's maps, several of which are reproduced in these pages. Dickinson and Shosteck knew of one another in the 1930s—perhaps they even considered reviving and collaborating on the 1918 Walk Book that was then still in Dickinson's possession. One of their mutual Washington friends wrote to Dickinson in 1934 that he had heard from Shosteck and was enclosing his note related to his *Washington Post*–sponsored walks. Dickinson included this letter referring to Shosteck in his album of drawings left to the Library of Congress a decade later.

Windy Run waterfall, the Potomac toward Chain Bridge, May 1918.

Windy Run appears just above Spout Run on Shosteck's map, at left, and today borders the George Washington Parkway. At some point in its long history as a quarry site, it was known as Little Italy for the workers who settled there in shacks. Windy Run's stones were used in many Washington buildings.

Chain Bridge

Chain Bridge, Washington, DC's first bridge over the Potomac, remains the public's favorite bridge and today serves as a principal commuter route for Virginians coming to the city. At the foot of Pimmit Run and a strategic location during the Civil War, Chain Bridge, in its eight incarnations, has witnessed more than two hundred years of local history. The first, covered-timber "Little Falls Bridge" was completed in 1797 and charged a crossing toll of three cents to pedestrians and eight cents to man and horse. It collapsed in 1804, and its replacement washed away in flood waters within six months of opening. In 1820, the third bridge went up and was named Chain Bridge because "Two chains made from one and one quarter inch wrought iron bars were suspended from massive stone towers at either shore and supported a wooden slab deck. Each link in the chain was four feet long."[34] Although this bridge soon succumbed to high waters, all subsequent replacements continued to bear the Chain Bridge name. The fourth bridge, of similar design, endured more than twenty years. The fifth bridge of 1840 lasted only a dozen years. The sixth bridge (1852–1870) was built adjacent to the old site on stone piers that support today's bridge. The Army Corps of Engineers' wrought-iron truss bridge of 1874 lasted until 1938, though it was closed in 1927 for major repairs. The eighth and last bridge opened in 1939. The old piers were enlarged to support a wider and taller bridge with three traffic lanes and two pedestrian sidewalks.[35]

Few traces of early settlements and structures at either end of Chain Bridge remain, but historians have studied and recorded this information in detail. On the Virginia side, the first development of the area began in 1719, when Thomas Lee (1690–1750) obtained the Langley tract of nearly 3,000 acres between Great Falls and Little Falls. Lee opened a grist mill and tobacco inspection warehouse at Pimmit Run, and his associate, Francis Awbrey, organized a ferry service along with an ordinary, or hotel. Between 1794 and 1805, new investors in the property developed a granary, grist mill, brewery, and blacksmith's shop. Again the land changed hands, and between 1816 and 1821, under the proprietorship of Edgar Patterson, the Chain Bridge location on the Virginia side "may have been among the busiest 200 feet of shoreline on the Potomac, with ships from Liverpool taking on tobacco and scows moving out 300 barrels of flour every two days. Consignments of woolen goods and three-point blankets

The high, precipitous escapment on the Virginia shore, along the base of which runs the swift, dark river, is broken at frequent intervals by hanging valleys, down which rush small but boisterous streams to drop far over into the river below. —Albert W. Atwood, *National Geographic,* 1945

Chain Bridge with the Palisades in the background, ca. 1920–1924. Photo by Martin Gruber, courtesy Smithsonian Institution Archives, SIA2010-2058.

from the mills—considered better than English woolens— were going aboard scows for the Georgetown market."[36] Rock from the cliffside was quarried from Patterson's day through 1938.

In August 1814, when the British burned Washington, Chain Bridge witnessed the flight of government auditor Stephen Pleasanton who carried precious documents, including the Declaration of Independence, to a mill on Pimmit Run, the first stop of his escape. During the Civil War, Fort Marcy and Fort Ethan Allen defended the bridge. Each night some of the span's flooring was removed to prevent attack.[37]

Chain Bridge
above Washington.

Chain Bridge from Little Falls, 1918.

chain Bridge
from little Falls
1918

The Rambler

Selections from "The Rambler" columns published in the *Evening Star* in the early twentieth century offer detailed descriptions of the local landscape and its inhabitants, which often complement Dickinson's sketches from the same period. Dickinson and J. Harry Shannon, the Rambler, met as a result of Dickinson's excursions for his proposed Walk Book. Shannon guided Dickinson to Prospect Rock and probably showed him other locations. (See pages 50–51 for photographs of their meeting.)

*Harry Shannon, "The Rambler," ca. 1915.
Courtesy the Historical Society of
Washington, DC.*

WITH THE RAMBLER

Pimmet Run

After crossing the water span and coming to the gray-dust road on the Virginia side, wooden steps lead down to a rocky ledge, and from [there] improvised steps of rough and irregularly placed stones will carry you down, if you are sure-footed, to the water's edge. It is a favorite place with fisher people, and a popular place with swimmers, though here among the rocks and the swift current and the eddies a good many men and boys have lost their lives. Here Pimmet run rushes into the river.... The Palisades have been gouged out here so there is quite a space between the river and the tree-topped cliffs. Among the quarry debris are the ruins of the foundation and piers formerly supporting a big stone-crushing plant. Down through the quarry and over the loose but heavy rocks Pimmet run foams.

If you will climb back to the gray-dust road you will note the steep high hill on the right, and past the first bend in that gray road, which is the beginning of the Leesburg Pike, a road, a-grown in grass and weeds and small shrubbery, leads up the hill. On the top you come upon the ruins of a building that was a landmark for a good many years. It was a hotel [High View Hotel], or a road-side resort, and, like so many places of that character, it had its golden days and its days of repentance and shabbiness. Its prosperity waned, it became a dilapidated old building, and then it fell prey to a fire. —The Rambler, *Evening Star,* June 27, 1915

WITH THE RAMBLER

On Conduit Road and Canal Road

On the right of the Conduit road [today's MacArthur Boulevard] you will come upon a square guide post set vertically in the ground and inscribed on one side "Conduit road" and on the other "Chain Bridge road." The road to the right leads to the high land north of the river. In the northeast angle of the two roads there is a small pebbledash church with a black sign lettered in gilt telling that it is St. David's Chapel, St. Alban's parish. At this road junction is a modern dwelling in flower-planted grounds and also an old and comfortable house that has stood there since before the civil war.

On the left of the Conduit road at this point one will notice a path bordered by cedar trees that leads down toward the river. The distance between the lines of cedars is the width of a road, but only a footpath runs between them. It is a stony way, washed by many rains. This lane crosses the electric railway tracks and then tumbles down a long and steep hill so washed that the basic rocks have been bared. Finally it enters the Canal road.

This little stretch of old and worn-down way is what is left of the early Chain Bridge road, the road by which people from the upper parts of Virginia traveled into Georgetown or into the old Maryland highways leading to the north, west and east.

This road led from the Chain bridge, or from the wooden bridges preceding Chain bridge...[and] entered the Rockville or old Frederick road at Tenleytown. Travelers bound for Georgetown would then follow the Rockville road southeastward to their destination. It was a roundabout way from the Little Falls crossing to Georgetown, but then it was the only road.

Before the bridging of the river at Little Falls there was a ferry, just as there was a ferry across the Eastern branch long before the building of the first bridge over that stream in 1795, and just as there was a ferry between the Virginia shore and the Maryland, or later the District side, long before the building of the aqueduct or the Aqueduct bridge.

There were at least two wooden bridges across the river at Little Falls before the building of the Chain bridge. They were both carried away by freshets, and when the bridge failed the ferry revived. It was thought that the freshet danger had been overcome when the Chain bridge was built. This was built after the pattern of a bridge that had been thrown over Jacobs creek near Uniontown, Pa. The Chain bridge was a suspension bridge, heavy chains being thrown over piers that rose twenty feet above the abutments. There were four of the chains, something after the fashion of the cables of the Brooklyn bridge. In the winter of 1840 the Chain bridge was swept away, that is, the chains and the wooden structure suspended from there went down stream. The abutments remained. The next bridge was of wood on stone piers. That was the bridge which connected two shores during the civil war, and which was finally superseded by the present bridge in 1874.

Here and there in the country north of the Conduit road may be seen a trace of the old road, but the only part obvious to the casual observer is the cedar-bordered path which leads from the Conduit road to the Canal road.—The Rambler, *Evening Star*, January 5, 1913

Scott's Run

Unbeknownst to most Washington-area residents is Scott's Run Nature Preserve, a jewel of a park known to locals as the Burling Tract, after its owner Edward Burling (1870–1966), co-founder of the downtown law firm Covington and Burling. This 336-acre wooded preserve is bounded by the Potomac River, the Capital Beltway, Georgetown Pike, and Scott's Run, and was the "bottom land" (the least valuable) of the old Ball estate when Burling purchased it in 1922. This area along Georgetown Pike is rich in settler history, and many place names relate to former landowners—Scott, Lee, Mackall, Trammel, Ball, and Tuberville, to list a few. Families intermarried and the estates subdivided. The pike's colorful heritage has been recorded by Betty Cooke (1913–2001), for whom a bridge near Swinks Mill is named.[38]

Until his death in 1966, Burling spent weekends enjoying his log cabin and picturesque retreat. His care for the land, which included selective tree-thinning, helped preserve the mature hardwood forest, a rare phenomenon on the East Coast, particularly in a metropolitan area where logging has occurred for hundreds of years. Also, the diversity of trees at Scott's Run, including beeches, oaks, hickories, cherries, and tuliptrees, has helped save the forest from disease. The creek trail from the parking lot leads to a grove of ancient hemlocks "whose ancestors migrated here during the last ice age."[39] Park regulars treasure the profusion of spring wildflowers—trailing arbutus (Mayflower), Virginia bluebells, and trillium—and also the variety of paths. One Fairfax County park manager has observed that "ruggedness is part of the charm of Scott's Run, creating almost a paradox between the rugged terrain and the fragile beauty of the blankets of wildflowers."[40]

Few visitors to the stream's lovely waterfall that flows into the Potomac know that the run's headwaters lie under Tyson's shopping mall parking lot. "Flowing east, through many business parks and condominium complexes, [the stream] ends its journey at the waterfall."[41]

After Burling's death, preserving the tract has presented a steady challenge. In the late 1960s, local citizens saved the land from the kind of development found along much of the Virginia shore above Chain Bridge. In 1969, Burling's heirs had negotiated the sale of the land to the developers Miller and Smith Associates for about $2 million. Plans included 309 luxury homes on 278 acres, preserving 58 acres along the riverfront palisades. The public reacted immediately, at first calling for an ecologically sound approach to the development and later for no development at all. The Fairfax County Park Authority, Planning Commission, and Board of Supervisors oversaw the year-long negotiations that ensued. Conservationists emphasized that clearing the land

The "Stone Gate" of "Scott's Run," the Potomac beyond.

The "Stone Gate"
of "Scott's Run"
The Potomac beyond

would not only endanger the flora and fauna but also cause serious erosion problems. Sewage disposal became another critical issue, because local treatment plants could not handle sewage for twelve hundred new residents.

The Interior Department proposed helping the Fairfax County Park Authority purchase the property for a park. Miller and Smith revised their plan, offering 58 acres to the Park Authority, which it accepted and promptly withdrew from the conflict. Citizens then looked for funds to match the Interior Department's $1.5 million purchase-assistance offer, but earlier pledges of support from the Nature Conservancy and State of Virginia had evaporated. Miller and Smith's revised plan was approved, setting off an appeals process that was not resolved until August 1970.

During the appeals process, high school students from Langley, McLean, and other neighboring communities collected signatures to create a park on the Burling Tract. A referendum in July 1970 to tax Dranesville citizens to help fund the proposed park met with success, causing Miller and Smith to up the sales price from $2.5 million to more than $6 million. A legal battle began, during which period Miller and Smith began bulldozing the land, then halted to negotiate a sales price of $3.6 million. The financers of the new park included the Interior Department in conjunction with the State of Virginia ($1.8 million) and county funds combined with a loan from a local developer-savior, Garfield Kass (the matching $1.8 million).[42]

Today, visitors to the park enjoy its trails and the spectacular sight of the stream cascading over jagged rocks into the Potomac. After the rippling stretch of Stubblefield Falls that follows, the Potomac then spreads into a serene pool where trees on both banks reflect in the water. Tawny rocks poke up from the water's surface as if the landscape of another planet. Their sunbaked color is actually a mud coating. Ducks and blue heron perch on the rocks in harmony with the universe. Enveloped in such a beautiful setting, few visitors realize the park's vulnerability. Just downstream the hazy framework of the American Legion Bridge—carrying the Capital Beltway—sweeps over a narrow neck in the river, a reminder of the bustling metropolitan environment pressing in on the area's parks. Funds are scarce for staff to administer Scott's Run; storm run-off pollutes the creek, in which people continue to swim even though swimming is banned; dog owners ignore the leash laws; and poachers dig up rare wildflowers.[43]

WITH THE RAMBLER

At Scott's Run

Scott's run pours into the Potomac six miles above the Chain bridge. Its numerous feeders rise in the country northeast of the Alexandria and Leesburg turnpike in the vicinity of Tyson Cross Roads and Peach Grove hill. It flows north, passing to the west of Lewinsville, crosses the Leesburg and Georgetown turnpike at Swink's mill, at the west base of Prospect hill. Then, for a mile, it flows in increasing volume through fine wild woods, and, plunging into a deep gorge which it has cut for itself during the course of many centuries, it foams in a number of cascades and leaps off a cliff. Then it joins the river. The junction of Scott's run and the river is called Stubblefield Falls, a point in the environs of Washington known to some fishermen and to the dwellers in the country tributary to Scott's run.

Where the great river rushes past the mouth of Scott's run a few jagged gray rocks jut above the surface and the troubled water shows that rock masses lie not far below the surface. The water whirls and eddies furiously there and at seasons of low water the obstructing rock masses cause a cascade in the river. Now whether that is "Stubblefield Falls" or whether Stubblefield Falls is the point within the gorge of Scott's run where the waters plunge over a cliff the Rambler does not now know. Nobody lives nearby and in that rocky spot where the run roared through its gorge the Rambler met no man to ask a question of.

North of the pike and along the east side of the run the rock hills and splendid woods are owned, according to the last survey examined by the Rambler, by the Langley Land Company. For a thousand yards north of the pike and on the west side of the run the land is that of the R. D. Evans estate and from the north line of that property to the Potomac river is another large tract belonging to the Langley Land Company.

The easiest way to get into this interesting country is to leave the line of the electric railway that runs to Great Falls on the Virginia side of the river at a stop called Hytaffer. Technically that stop is called a station, because a waiting shed and a platform are there....

[A] path leads through the woods following the course of the run. Half a mile along this path brings you to a grove or clump of hemlock trees. Some of them are magnificent specimens, being about eighty feet tall, with trunks a foot and a half thick and foliage bright and refreshingly green. The Rambler knows that many persons interested in such matters believe that the native hemlocks growing nearest to Washington are a few poor specimens at Prospect Rock, a mile west of the mouth of Scott's run. Beyond these hemlocks one catches sight of masses of gneiss, a foundation rock of this part of the world, and this begins to tell the story of how deeply Scott's run has worn its way beneath what centuries ago was the surface of the earth. Soon the run makes a sharp turn, enters the rocky gorge which the Rambler mentioned in the beginning, and, looking through this gorge, one glimpses, about 400 yards away, the yellow, turbid Potomac.

The field of view permitted by the mouth of the gorge is a small one, and only a trifling patch of the Potomac is visible, but pass through the gorge or climb the rock hills on either side and an extensive view of the river east and west is obtained. Far to the north and beyond the river, small, fast-moving vehicles mark the line of the Conduit road between Cabin John and Great Falls.

Along the bed of the stream within the gorge are immense boulders tossed there by a force which makes one's head swim to contemplate. Where, in this dim place, there is a root hold for a tree, that tree is a hemlock, and on the steep slopes above the gorge hundreds of hemlocks grow. Here is a spot of grandeur and wild beauty, a place of scenic majesty, close to Washington, but which relatively few Washington people have ever seen.
—The Rambler, *Evening Star,* April 16, 1916

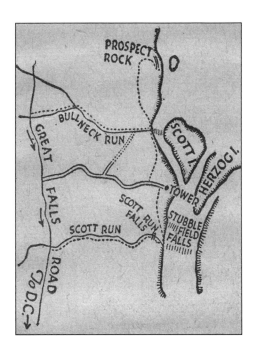

Prospect Rock. **Robert Shosteck,**
Guide to Trails around Washington.
© Robert Shosteck, 1937.

Prospect Rock

Robert L. Dickinson discovered the lower Potomac's wonder of the world: Prospect Rock, a jutting promontory that affords a three-sided panorama of the meandering river some 230 feet below. Close by is Bull Neck Run with its traces of nineteenth-century gold-mining activity. For a brief period gold prospecting flourished on both sides of the river, but Prospect Rock's name undoubtedly comes from its commanding view.

The only early-twentieth-century writer tramping and blazing Potomac trails and then recording the natural world and genealogical discoveries he encountered along the way was the *Evening Star*'s "Rambler." Several local libraries have J. Harry Shannon's collected articles on microfilm, but many are illegible and deserve a fresh effort at preservation. A good collection of Shannon's photographs remains, and the two pictures on pages 51–52 document Dickinson's meeting with the Rambler, who acted as Dickinson's guide the day he sketched and picnicked at Prospect Rock. Dickinson's title "The Introduction" probably refers to that meeting, as it shows Dickinson, the Rambler, and Mrs. Agnew shaking hands at the rock, but the title could also be a play on words, for Dickinson's sketch introduces the rock and its sweeping vista. The curl of smoke in the picture is likely a campfire for a picnic lunch suggested by the second sketch of "The Cook," who is identified at the top of the drawing as "Mrs. Agnew, Bureau [of] Standards professor's wife."

Although today the landscape surrounding Prospect Rock is almost as wild as it was in 1918, a contemporary house occupies the site, with a quiet Japanese garden leading to the Olympian rock. This is the last home on a long, private lane developed during the 1970s, when public access to Prospect Rock ended.

A contemporary view of
Prospect Rock. © 2004 Ernie
Brooks, Rock Creek Images.

The Introduction,
Prospect Rock, the
Potomac, Mar. 1918.

The
Introduction

Prospect Rock
The Potomac Mar 1918.

Probably Mrs. Agnew and Dickinson,
photographed by the Rambler the day
Dickinson sketched Prospect Rock.
Courtesy the Historical Society of
Washington, DC.

Dickinson sketching on Prospect Rock. Courtesy the Historical Society of Washington, DC.

WITH THE RAMBLER

At Prospect Rock

Prospect Rock is a rugged, rude-built tower on the Virginia side of the Potomac river between Washington and Great Falls, and is a viewpoint reached by many persons, though the number of pilgrims measured by the whole population of the capital is negligible.

No man's hand played any part in the building of this tower. It is older than any work of man. When the water which we call the Potomac ripped and tore a channel from the Alleghenies to the sea it left standing this castle of rock, and other waters rushing to join the Potomac have washed deep and steep ravines on either side and have littered the slopes of these dark chasms with great bowlders, all jumbled and heaped and strewn around as though some mad or sportive giant had there built himself a house and then had thrown it down.

The country for miles around the rock is closely wooded. No matter how you approach the place from the land side, your way will lay through woods wherein grow all the trees, wild shrubs and wild flowers of this latitude, and in the thickets, the dense woods and the relatively open woods nearly all the birds—permanent residents, summer residents, summer migrants and winter migrants—may be found, with the result that this territory is a favorite hunting ground for the numerous true naturalists and the more numerous near-naturalists of Washington.

As all who live or wander in that part of the country around Washington know, the land between the Leesburg Pike [today's Georgetown Pike], which leads west from Chain bridge, and the river is tree-grown, with here and there a clearing which in most cases shows signs of returning to the forest state. In these woods, especially along the leaf-green and rock-gray palisades, is an occasional permanent home, bungalow or "camp," but they are few, and it may be that following one of the many dim and faint trails that lead through this vast tree-tract you will travel miles without coming upon a habitation....

Prospect Rock is about one mile north of the pike and about two miles north of the electric railway. One of the features of the country is that it is eroded with ravines, most of them deep with steep sides which are generally matted with that evergreen variously called laurel, or spoonwood, or calico bush, but which is set down in the books of botanists as Kalmia latifolia, one of the most popular and beautiful shrubs. Nearly every Washingtonian who goes into the woods brought back to the city during the last two weeks of May and the first week of June armfuls of these blossoms....

Through a number of the ravines streams rush and the water has worn down the land to the basic rock of the region, Carolina gneiss. The bottom of the ravines is bowlder-strewn and in many parts of their course the streams splash and foam through gorges into which because of the sheerness of their sides, their depth and the shade of trees little sunlight enters. Those branches passing through the woods and entering the Potomac in the neighborhood of Prospect Rock are Scott's run, Bullneck run and Difficult run.

Along these streams are many mill-sites, for, because of the volume and fall of the water, this was a milling territory when the milling of grain was a neighborhood industry. The ruin of dams, vague traces of millraces and the overgrown fragments of mills may be found, and on Scott's run, where the pike crosses, stands the frame shell of a mill which turned its wheels and ground corn and wheat up to about eighteen years ago. This is Swink's mill, and the miller of that name still lives across the road from the old mill in a venerable and picturesque house washed so white that it dazzles in the sunshine except where its walls are veiled with wisteria and Virginia creeper.

There are various ways of reaching Prospect Rock, but last Sunday the Rambler left the electric car at the station bearing the unusual name of Hytaffer. At that place the iron road passes through a deep cut and a wagon road passes overhead on a wooden bridge. Steep steps lead from the iron to the dirtroad. It was early morning and the air was sweet with the fragrance of pine....

On the right is low, wooded country, just taking on the form of a valley, and through that is flowing Scott's run, not yet having reached the wild and rocky part of its course. But the descent both of the dirt road and of the branch is steady, and half a mile farther on road and branch [they] are running side by side through rocks and trees.

Where the water of the branch is especially frothy and noisy you see a jumbled mass of rocks and rotting timber, and you know that there was once a mill dam. A depression through the shrubbery tells that once it was a mill race, and if you explore a laurel thicket you will come upon heaps of rocks that were once Ball's mill—a mill that was grinding about a century ago and which ceased to grind about the time of the breaking out of the civil war.

Following the road and the creek you come to the Leesburg Pike, where it climbs down and up across the valley of Scott's run. Swink's mill stands at the southwest corner of the road junction, and the home of the former miller, E. F. Swink, stands at the southeast corner.

Mr. Swink told the Rambler that the mill was built at that place a few years after the close of the civil war, grinding grain from the fields that had poured their golden tribute between the stones of Ball's mill, which stood farther up the run and which had ended its toll with the coming of the war. Mr. Swink said that the present mill had been built and set in operation by a man named Welsh. It was, of course, known as Welsh's mill. Later it became McGarrity's mill, Albert McGarrity having assumed control of its destinies. Twenty-three years ago it became Swink's mill, but profits on grinding wheat and corn declined and the wheels of the old mill ceased to turn.

The place where the Leesburg Pike, the Swink mill road and Scott's run meet is a low, damp and woody region. There is a hilltop clearing, or a hillside clearing above the mill in the direction of Washington and in a log house in that clearing lives Henrietta Carter.

The pike crosses the run on a bridge and then climbs a steep hill with wide and dark laurel-tangled ravines on both sides, while the run boils and splashes on its way toward the Potomac, which it enters between Yellow Rock and Stubblefield Falls near Jackson Island which, before it was Jackson Island, was Turkey Island, a name that endures today among the oldest settlers in the region.

But on this trip you do not want to follow the run. Your way leads westward on the pike and after climbing the hill, after crossing the bridge, you come to a gray stone wall by the side of the pike and on the right hand. A well, covered by a quaint rustic house, stands close by the road. There is a lawn, gay with patches of bright flowers, and above these rise very old black locust trees. In the background is a comfortable and retired-looking house. It is around this house and among the locust trees that part of Jackson ruins stand and about which the Rambler has previously written.

At the west corner of the low stone wall by the side of the pike a lane leads off to the right and toward the river.

That is your way. Following this and veering to the left wherever the trail forks you pass down a stony hill and come upon a fine spring. The shade here and the cold, safe water will invite you to rest. From the spring the road continues down grade through thick woods with a plentiful undergrowth of greenery and you soon come to a stream which resembles Rock creek from Broad branch to the Military road, before Beech [sic] drive was built.

The road along which you have come fords the stream and leads along its left bank in the direction of the river, but it is now become a faint woodland trace and you should not follow it if you would come to Prospect Rock by the quickest and easiest route. The rocky stream which you have crossed is called Bull Neck run. Why it has that name, or by whom it was given, the Rambler does not know. The origin of country or place names is usually interesting, but...[often hard to determine].

On the western or farther side of Bull Neck run rises a high, steep hill, all in woods. A dim little path leads up, being first to the left and then to the right. Not enough feet have pressed this woodland path to make it distinct, but with a fair measure of woods sense you can follow it. A breath-taking climb brings you to the top into a forest road and this road leads by deep excavations and the red earth and rocks' quartz and iron-stone thrown out on these pits and trenches make mounds like giant ant hills. The forest road was made while these excavations were being dug. It is a Potomac gold mine. Men, urged on by great hopes, toiled there. There are many, many "gold mines" in the hills that border the Potomac river, both on the Maryland and the Virginia side.

You continue along this forest trace now heading west and another faint trace [heads] northward through the trees and laurel. At the fork of these trails is a [young] oak tree and at about the height of a man's eye a piece of stout but weather-worn fabric is tied around the tree like a bandage. Once that bandage was a bright red and it was tied around the tree to tell pilgrims destined for Prospect Rock to take the right hand trail.

This trail heads you along the backbone of a ridge that steadily grows narrower. Great ravines falling away on the right and the left are steadily deepening. The roar of water comes to your ears. Through the foliage and the branches of the trees you catch glimpses of the river far below and the wooded hills on the Maryland side. A few rods bring you to the end of the trail and the [place] of a pile of gray rocks. The place is Prospect Rock, and climbing upon the rocks, you have such a view of the river, the woods and hills to the north, the east and the west as an eagle might envy.—The Rambler, *Evening Star,* June 20, 1915

Prospect Rock over the Potomac,
March 1918, the Cook. At top:
Mrs. Agnew, Bureau [of]
Standards professor's wife.

PROSPECT ROCK
over the Potomac
March 1918
The Cook

Difficult Run is a very rocky and picturesque ravine…. The proximity to Great Falls, the scenic beauty, and the abundance of wild flowers make this trail very popular with hikers. —Robert Shosteck, *The Potomac Trail Book*

Wild country for tramping: the Potomac where Difficult Run comes in below Great Falls. Great rocks.

Dickinson's hand-drawn map of recreational spots along the Potomac includes trail directions to swimming holes, some literally large potholes. Close to Difficult Run, Dickinson describes a trail leading to Black Pool, also known as Black Pond. In Dickinson's day, hikers would circle Yellow Pool, follow rock cairns to view points, and then "at the bungalow," fork left to Black Pond. Buzzard's Roost (page 58) lies west of these pools, more or less across the river from Widewater.

Dickey's Tavern

Although Dickey's Tavern began as Mrs. Meyer's Tavern in the late 1700s, the Dickey family ran it for several generations into the 1930s. The building burned down in June 1950. Famed for having served dinner to every president from George Washington to Theodore Roosevelt, Dickey's was known for its fish dinners—shad and bass—and in the early 1900s for Jane Dickey's fried chicken. At various times it was also an inn, and in its early years, a hostelry for canal boatmen. Built as part of Matildaville, Dickey's was the town's only structure to survive into the twentieth century. Intended to support George Washington's Patowmack Canal Company, Matildaville was named for "Light-Horse Harry" Lee's young wife Matilda, who died shortly before the town was founded. Lee built it expecting the town to prosper as a result of the canal company commerce. Even before the Virginia canal system closed in 1830, Matildaville failed to flourish, though it briefly witnessed flour and saw mills and an iron foundry. Today, the remains of Dickey's stone chimney can be visited in Great Falls Park, Virginia.

Dickey's Tavern and members of the Dickey family, ca. 1900. James Watt Collection, Fairfax County Public Library Photographic Archive.

Dicky's [sic], below Great Falls, log cabin.

Washington lived along the river, traveled its waters, and even fished it commercially.... I hope he also felt its lulling charm when you ship your paddles on a summer afternoon and drift with a lazy current. The world slows until the panorama of fields and forests seems to float by while you and time stand still. Stately herons feed and fly in slow motion. The river seduces with a deceptive gentleness as it licks at the banks and gurgles past rocks and logs. —Wilbur E. Garrett, *National Geographic*, June 1987

Buzzard's Roost & the great potholes on the Potomac.

Trails

Trails are not dust and pebbles on a hill,
Nor even grass and wild buds by a lake;
Trails are adventure and a hand to still
The restless pulse of life when men would break
Their minds with weight of thinking.
Trails are peace,
The call to dreams, the challenge to ascent;
Trails are the brisk unfolding of release
From bitterness and from discouragement.
Trails are the random writing on the wall
That tells how every man, grown tired at heart
Of things correct and ordered, comes to scrawl
His happy hour down and goes to start
Life over with new eagerness and zest.
Who breaks a trail finds labor that is rest.
—Helen Frazee-Bower, *Bulletin,* Potomac
Appalachian Trail Club, October 1939

The Castle Passage in Cleft Island.
Potomac: The Island of the Lake, 1918.

A canal pattern
[the C&O Canal].

River Camps
and Cabin John

River Camps and Cabin John

Summer Camps along the Potomac

Roaring Camp, Happy Rest, Selger Camp, Fracker Camp, Trammel's, and other summer camps once lined both sides of the Potomac above and below Washington. And outdoor clubs—the Mohican, Alpine, Wanderlusters, and Rambler Pastime—offered communal activities inspired by the capital's great waterway. Recreational use of the river continues today, and some of the early clubs still exist, including the Sycamore Island Canoe Club, the Washington Canoe Club, and the Potomac Boat Club. Other organizations have formed—the Potomac Appalachian Trail Club, now about eighty years old; the Sierra Club; and county and city hiking, biking, birding, and boating groups. Despite the river's continuous recreational use, many changes have come. First, few people swim in the Potomac anymore—swimming is now forbidden in the metropolitan area because of dangerous currents that claim victims every year, and today public pools are available. Second, urban dwellers no longer camp out along the shores on sweltering summer nights, or for entire summers, as they did until the 1930s. Documentation of this unique tradition in Washington is scarce. Robert L. Dickinson left evidence of Trammel's and other rustic river resorts north of Great Falls both in his drawings and on his hand-drawn map. The Rambler recorded glimpses of the summer-camp landscape in his columns, partially reprinted here. Histories of the C&O Canal and Great Falls occasionally refer to the camps, and today's old-timers recall their parents' camping stories. Archival photographs document the tents, hammocks, and rustic outdoor kitchens of family campgrounds, and Dickinson's drawings capture the look of the more established sites where patrons paid for lodging and meals. Wealthier residents took trains out of town to fancy resort hotels. But many middle-class Washingtonians who desired a summer retreat found few obstacles to setting up camp along the Potomac. They commuted to work via the trolley, electric railway, or boats heading downstream. Many campers returned to the same spot—their camp—each summer.

In 1923, only five years after Dickinson's sketches of Potomac summer camps, a *National Geographic* article described the river as being "flecked with canoes, launches, and rowboats—literally with thousands of canoes if it be a pleasant week-end afternoon. Between the whirlpool of 'Little Falls' and the decrepit wharves that betoken the former importance of Georgetown as a river port is Washington's aquatic playplace supreme."[1] A proliferation of refreshment stands and even floating dance floors added to the resort flavor on the C&O Canal side. On the steeper Virginia side arose "a veritable city of shacks and tents, with landings as close as those of a Venetian street. A kindly construction company has allowed campers 'to pick their sites,' and these 'squatter rights' are rigidly regulated by a sort of town-meeting government improvised each summer by campers themselves."[2]

Old-timer Dusty Rhodes (born in 1912) remembered Washington lawyer Jim Birch's summer campsite on the Virginia shore. "Jim paddled his canoe to the Potomac Boat Club in Georgetown, climbed the steps up over the canal, and caught a streetcar to the Investment Building downtown. Several lawyers did that." Gilbert Grosvenor's *National Geographic* article of March 1928 elaborates on Dusty's story: "Many persons who have to work in Washington all summer move their whole families to tents and shacks on the banks of the river above the city [Maryland side], where they live through the hot months. On Sunday mornings they attend church under the trees."[3] According to the article, white-collar workers shaved at the river's edge before paddling down to Georgetown to catch the streetcar to work. "Few great cities are so situated that their people may enjoy the pleasures and benefits of camp life during the summer and still continue to work regularly," Grosvenor wrote.[4]

Who knows for how long, but probably for decades, the C&O Canal Company permitted camping on its unused shoreline between the canal and river. Old-timers believe that private landowners also invited friends to set up camps on their property during the summertime. Those who could afford it, or who didn't want such a rustic experience, could stay at lodges such as Trammel's. The Baltzley family, owners of Glen Echo, also rented out campgrounds with luxury tents and photographed summer scenes there (see pages 90–91). When the C&O Canal closed in 1924, the free camping tradition continued until the Roosevelt administration purchased the bankrupt company in September 1938. The Depression years brought true squatter settlements to the shoreline, so that part of the purchase agreement included removing "all occupants of the property other than existing water leasees," the latter of whom numbered about 180 tenants.[5]

Campers for 2 miles along the Potomac above Washington, 1917.

Campers for 2 miles
along the Potomac
above Washington 1917

*Potomac, Great Falls—these river
cabins, 25 cents a night—good food.*

The shore and the dining room at
Trammel's above Great Falls, 1918.

Like Adirondack camps—
five miles of adventurous
canoe-water above the dam,
Potomac, Great Falls.

Like adirondack Camps — five miles
of adventurous canoe-water above the dam
Potomac - Great Falls

A typical family campsite along the Potomac, below Washington on the Virginia side, ca. 1905. Photos courtesy Jane Yeatman Spangler.

Dickinson's Potomac map, found at the back of the book, documents summer life on the Potomac. His calligraphic notations cover the map and demonstrate his remarkable degree of touring, given his brief eighteen months in Washington for the war effort. In the map's far left corner on the river's Virginia side, Dickinson has written: "To lake above dam, to boats and camps," and just below this: "Tent City." At the end of Difficult and Pawpaw Runs, in the shallow shore water, he advises: "swim." His notation "c" indicates campsites, and on the Maryland side he has marked the ferry landings for Trammel's and River Bend camps. Historic maps show Trammel's Island as today's Beall's Island, north of Great Falls. It is possible the Rambler guided Dickinson on his river camp excursions, for the Rambler's camp articles appeared at about the same time as Dickinson's drawings and have been excerpted here.

WITH THE RAMBLER

A well worn trail leads from Great Falls north along the Virginia shore. For half a mile it is broad and well defined and then for another half mile it is considerably narrower, though still clearly defined. Thence on to the Great Bend it is a haphazard sort of trail, which has been marked over the big stones and through the close-grown shrubbery by the feet of fishermen and these adventurous walkers who are lured and not appalled by the call of the wild.... Beyond that point the trail has been marked by men and women going as far up as Trammell's, some to fish or otherwise refresh themselves, and some to be ferried over the river above the dam which impounds and deflects a part of the Potomac into the Washington aqueduct. Above that point a few people pass along bound for Dr. Ladd's house, which he calls "River Bend Camp," or for camps of the Powhatan and Mid-River Canoe clubs.... Above the falls are beautiful scenes and good people.... It is a region of peace and great beauty where... the roadside houses are bowered in fruit blossoms and the gardens are gay with flowers.

Uncle Jimmy Trammell. Since passed away at 82. Had lived in the Great Falls neighborhood all those years. His father and grandfather and grandfather had lived in that part of Fairfax county and the Trammell line reached back to Indian days. —The Rambler, *Evening Star,* May 12, 1918

* * *

There are several paths that invite the traveler in the same direction, but they all converge upon the broad and tortuous—not torturous—way which, if followed, will conduct one to the rustic camps and boat sheds that snuggle among the trees between the green and gray bluff and the glistening river above the [Great Falls] dam.... When you come to Trammells you land in a region of canoes and fish stories. Uncle "Tant" Trammell sits under the wide-spreading sycamores and native elms and recounts memories that he has garnered during his eighty-nine years of life on the upper river and the country beside it. John Trammell is also there, but John belongs to the generation of motor boats, telephones, electric lights, trolley cars and such modern contraptions. Nearby, bowered in foliage, is the camp of L. H. Harris of the Treasury. When he is not dealing in money by the million he is catching small-mouth bass.

One is impressed with the frequency with which the names Trammell, Gunnell and Rollins occur in the environs of Washington. These are among the old families of Virginia....

The first of the Trammells in this part of Virginia whose memory is preserved in the traditions of the old inhabitants was Dr. Trammell. He had a son named Washington Trammell and a daughter who married "Doddy" Jenkins.... Then there was another Trammell, a son of Washington Trammell, the son of Dr. Trammell. His name was Fielden Trammell. He lived on the old Conn farm at Great Falls, Conn being a big landholder in that neighborhood, who gave his name to Conn Island, the large wooded island above the falls. The original Conn house is standing and is the present home of Anthony Cowley. Fielden Trammell married Miss Frances Rollins and their children were George, Martha, William, James and John, who are dead, and Fielden Davis Trammell, who lives with John Trammell, son of George, and Thomas Trammell, who lives in Forrestville, Va. William Trammell, who married Miss Dickey, had as children, Virginia, Mittie Lee, Annie, William, James, Mary, Guy, and Elizabeth.... The Dickey family is another of the old Great Falls families.—The Rambler, *Evening Star,* May 19, 1918

WITH THE RAMBLER

Take any car bound westward and up the riverside any Sunday in summer time or fair days in winter and from morning until afternoon you will be sure to see picnickers in khaki, middles and sweaters, with fishing poles, oil cans, suit cases or baskets of provisions, piling in anywhere and everywhere and dominating serious folk in civilized Sabbath garb and frame of mind with their merry persiflage.

From Chain Bridge to Cabin John or beyond the disembarking continues, sometimes in a solitary nature taker alighting, and sometimes a round dozen men and maids. Follow any of the paths or many flights of steps down to the canal, cross a lock, Sycamore Island bridge or in a ferry and you will be amazed at the summer resort character of the lands along the river.

Up the canal, in canoes, rowboats and launches; up the towpath, on foot, and down the hill from the cars come the merry campers to their shacks or bunga-lows (some are even of brick—that is, the houses, not the campers) for a camp dinner.

[Along the Virginia side] Close to the dam at Little Falls is "Roaring Camp," named for its proximity to the noisy water rather than the character of its owner.... Not far above is another camp, and then above this is a shingled cottage with a stone chimney built by journeymen carpenters and stone-masons, and after a honeymoon that was spent there the place was dubbed "Happy Rest."...[Climbing on] one soon comes to an old camp where the remains of rustic tables and benches of various sizes and what was once an old tent floor tell the tale of a comfortable outing place until two copperhead snakes were killed under the tent floor. Continue on and upward and at last you see a bungalow of halved logs with the bark on, a peaked roof, side porches, sleeping and cooking rooms, and L's jutting from either side at the back. Two oak trees form the front corner posts. If any one is at home, hammocks are swinging among the oaks toward the river. The water is glimpsed between the trees— plainly when the leaves are gone—and the roar of the falls is heard subdued to just the right music for soft conversation in the hammocks or for sound sleep at night.

[Near this campsite, toward the river were] the Delano-Smith camp...the Seifritz camp, where there is a piano in the bungalow, the camp of Frank Bright and Richard Oberly, the Selger Camp, the K.K.K. camp [possibly Ku Klux Klan].... Opposite these camps are the Washington Canoe Club on High Island, the Mahoney camp, the Fracker camp, the place of Dr. Isaac Stone, and the camp of the Washington Normal School. —The Rambler, *Evening Star,* ca. 1918

Here begins the 19-mile stairway which lowers the Potomac 190 feet from the Piedmont to the coastal plain. The steps are called falls—Seneca, Great, Difficult, Yellow, Stubblefield, and Little; but with the exception of the second, they might more correctly be described as sharp rapids. —Ralph Gray, *National Geographic*, August 1948

Pennyfield Lock, below Seneca.

Seneca

Although Washington lacks Rome's ancient ruins for a Sunday outing, a visit to Seneca, just off River Road, offers some satisfaction. When Dickinson sketched the river near Seneca, the canal still produced some commerce, but today this bucolic landscape shows hardly a trace of its colorful C&O Canal history (see page 23). The adventurer can walk beyond the old aqueduct and Riley's lockhouse to discover, amid dense undergrowth, the inspiring ruins of the Seneca stonecutting mill, built in 1837. Those visitors familiar with the Smithsonian Castle (1847–1849) will recognize the dark-red sandstone blocks of this looming, majestic relic. The Castle's stones were quarried and cut here, and an overgrown path leads to the abandoned quarry itself. Seneca's stones also contributed to the Cabin John Bridge and portions of many buildings and residences in downtown Washington.

In the center of the ruined mill stands the channel that powered a waterwheel and later a turbine. The former saw "cut stone at the then astonishing rate of an inch an hour."[6] Imagine cutting thousands of stone blocks for the Smithsonian Castle. Near the mill, the canal widens to accommodate a turning basin, for Seneca was once the terminus for canal commerce. The pool and submerged loading dock can still be seen. Later, when Cumberland took over as the canal's terminus, Seneca became the changing station for mules.

Seneca's handsome, red-sandstone aqueduct was damaged in September 1971, when Seneca Creek "became a raging torrent and houses, boats, trees and other debris were torn loose upstream and thrown against the aqueduct," collapsing its west arch.[7] Seneca Creek State Park now encompasses this historic area, with the Mckee-Besher Wildlife Management Area preserve adjacent to it. Both parks afford superb birding opportunities.

Pennyfield Lock

A pleasant towpath walk below Seneca leads to Pennyfield Lock, where gentle light filters through a thick canopy of trees and the Potomac meanders peacefully. The clean air has a woodsy scent. No wonder President Grover Cleveland made Pennyfield Lock one of his summer retreats. According to lore, his frame house stood opposite the lock, and he and the lockkeeper, Mr. Pennyfield, became good friends, probably enjoying fishing together. Whenever President Cleveland departed for the White House, he always reminded Mr. Pennyfield to "stop by and see me when you come to town." One day Mr. Pennyfield, dressed in his only suit, presented himself at the White House, where a servant informed him the president was busy. Mr. Pennyfield told the servant to let the president know that Mr. Pennyfield had come to see him. A few minutes later, President Cleveland appeared, clapped Mr. Pennyfield on the back, and invited him to dinner. "They had a jolly old time discussing fishing, mutual Potomac friends, and canal news."[8] For those weekend strollers who also enjoy birding, the thirty-acre Dierssen Waterfowl Sanctuary abuts Pennyfield Lock.

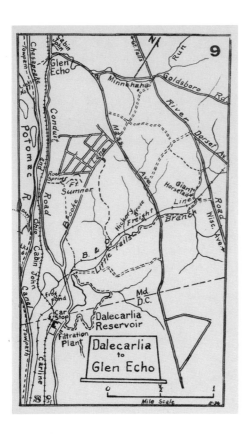

Dalecarlia to Glen Echo. **Robert Shosteck,** *Guide to Trails around Washington,* **© Robert Shosteck, 1937.**

Cabin John Bridge

Even without the remarkable Cabin John Bridge, the area along the Potomac River known as Cabin John would have endured the test of time with its mystique and devoted community. Over the centuries, many things combined to distinguish Cabin John, its name high on the list. From its rural days of a few homesteads to its recreational heyday at the turn of the twentieth century, when the Cabin John Hotel boomed, to its more recent helter-skelter development, Cabin John was and remains a rustic romantic enclave.

To some people, Cabin John's greatest environmental intrusion has been to the historic bridge, which now spans a highway. The bridge is an amazing stone structure, designed by Alfred L. Rives and built by Montgomery C. Meigs from 1853 to 1867, and in its day was the longest masonry arch bridge. Its high, beautiful arch was perfectly reflected in the creek's pool below it, inspiring Dickinson to capture the image. The wooded hillsides surrounding the bridge and overlooking a relatively peaceful stretch of the Potomac have also been compromised by property subdivision that appears unplanned. Abutting Cabin John's western edge at Carderock is the monstrous Naval Surface Warfare Center, better known by its older name, the David Taylor Model Basin, whose water-testing structure consumes a vast stretch of Potomac panorama. These intrusions on the picturesque setting have not affected Cabin John's appeal. It is still an outpost, still a devoted community; history marks it, and Washingtonians continue to escape on weekends to its riverside scenery and trails, only seven miles from Georgetown. What an observer from 1903 wrote about Cabin John's natural beauty holds true today: "Aside from the bridge itself, the creek that it crosses, the ravines and hills, the forests, the deep, shadowy glens and tangled wildwoods are in themselves deep objects of interest and beauty."[9]

The name Cabin John or possibly Captain John Creek (or Run) may derive from a mysterious hunting hermit with protective dogs who lived for several years on the hill above the stream. This story was passed down through several generations of Cabin John families, whose forefathers supposedly lived at the same time as the legendary, late-eighteenth-century John. The strange man was called John, John of the Cabin, and Captain John. Some Montgomery County records that predate the John of the Cabin story refer to the creek as Captain Johns Run or Branch. Thus, "Cabin John" is either a corruption of "Captain John" or "Johns" or a derivative of "John of the Cabin." Captain John Smith also has been proposed as a source for the name, for in 1608 he explored and mapped the Potomac River "as high as we could bote."[10] There also may have been a "Johns Cabin" inn at the junction of River Road and the creek, resulting in the place name, or a prominent Indian named John who lived by the creek and became known as John of the Cabin. To some locals Cabin John was a musician with a broken heart.

In the historic record, these stories often become entangled and new versions spin out. For instance, one story pertains to African American slaves who believed that after John's disappearance his ghost haunted the site.[11] A strand of this story has John as a pirate who hid his treasure by the bridge and then disappeared. But when the night wind was strong he returned to the area, and if spotted he disappeared in a flare of light. As a result, African Americans "would never cross the bridge after midnight, especially on a Saturday."[12] When the American Land Company began to develop Cabin John in 1912, new property owners received deeds that stated they would have to give the company "one-half interest in any treasure or articles of special value which may have been hidden on said lot or parcel by John of the Cabin." Even today a few Cabin John residents have deeds containing such wording.

Over decades, versions of the Cabin John story continued to be told. A Washington *Evening Star* article in 1913 blended all of them into one tall tale, citing for source material "the citizens of that community who got their information from their fathers, grandfathers and great-grandfathers":

> Before the capital city was located on the Potomac, Georgetown was simply a village, the highest point on the river for seagoing vessels, whence imports of all kinds were distributed north and west by wagon trains via two main highways which for many miles passed through dense forests. In those days the present property along Cabin John run was a secure hiding place. It was there that a crude man name "John" built a cabin by the creek or run, lived like a hermit and subsisted apparently on game, fish, nuts and wild plants.
>
> Large projecting stones served as sidewalls and a few poles inclosed the front, while brush, bark and sod formed the roof and completed this crude home. He was always very busy in the fall, and squirrel-like, stored away many bushels of winter food from the many large and prolific walnut, chestnut, and hickorynut trees along Cabin John run.
>
> One theory handed down by old inhabitants is that this life of privation and isolation was the aftermath of an unsatisfactory love affair in a distant state…. In course of time he was known as "John of the Cabin," and his domicile was called "cabin of John," but at a later date this was reduced to the simpler form, "Cabin John," and apparently by general consensus of the community, the creek took the name of "Cabin John run…."
>
> This strange man inhabited his humble hut for many years, shunning and avoiding everybody, claiming no neighbors except

Cabin John Bridge over Cabin John Creek, photographed by the Detroit Publishing Company, ca. 1900. Courtesy Library of Congress, Prints and Photographs Division.

Cabin John Bridge.

the rocks and trees, and no associates or companions except his gun and his fierce and fleet-footed dogs.... He scoured the surrounding fields and woods by day and night, his chief pleasure being trapping and running down the wily raccoon. He made his own clothes, and they were heavy and flowing garments of skins of wild animals caught or killed in the neighborhood. Because of these garments he had quite the appearance of a woman when some distance away. He avoided all kinds of companionship, but was never known to do an unkind or harmful act during all the years of his wild and lonely life.

At times curious persons ventured into the vicinity of the cabin and frequently they would hear music on some peculiar instrument, and sometimes he would sing songs and quaint and touching melodies in a foreign language, apparently referring to distant lands and one whose memory he cherished.

Another strange part of this melancholy story is that "John" disappeared as suddenly and as mysteriously as his first coming. The dogs deserted the rocky kennel, the clumsy cabin crumbled to dust, but there still remain to recall his memory "Cabin John run" and "Cabin John bridge."

It was during the time of slavery that "John" lived this hermit life, and the colored people in that part of the country feared him and looked upon him with superstitious awe. After his disappearance they claimed that his ghost or spirit could be seen in that community any dark or rainy Saturday night....

Sometime during the year 1825 a small piece of paper, faded with age, was found under a dilapidated grain bin in an old mill located on the banks of Cabin John run, in which the lines below were written in the English language, but the writing indicated the hand of a foreigner. Many think that "John" wrote and secreted the lines there before his disappearance, for it was his custom to come about the mill at times when he was not observed, apparently to pick up a few grains of corn and wheat....

> *When the last raccoon on the creek had been slain,*
> *It is said he jumped into the river again;*
> *As no name to the creek by the ancients was given,*
> *It was called "Cabin John" after he went to heaven.*

Another legend credits the same John with having quite a different reason for seeking solitude in this unknown retreat; it asserts that he was a retired pirate…hiding for the time being to hold and protect a large fortune gathered by foul means on the high seas. This theory is strengthened by the mystery which surrounds his every movement, and because his ultimate fate is unknown. No one can now tell whether John was grieving in solitude for some lost love or was guarding a vast treasure from a pirate ship, securely hidden among the rocks and trees.[13]

A crumbling, nineteenth-century photographer's brochure that tells the same story about an 1825 poem under an old mill's grain bin provides an extra verse to the poem:

"John of the Cabin"—a curious wight—
Sprang out of the river one dark stormy night:
He built a warm hut in a lonely retreat,
And lived many years upon fishes and meat.

When the last lone raccoon on the creek he had slain,
It is said he jumped into the river again.
As no name to the creek by the ancients was given,
It was called "Cabin John" after John went to Heaven.[14]

A 1903 brochure titled "Picturesque Cabin John," by J. H. Wilson Marriott, contains a poem by the author:

In the long ago past, there mysteriously came
An odd looking creature, whom none knew his name;
He fished and he hunted, but troubled no one,
Was contented and happy with dogs and his gun.

After spending awhile in this beautiful spot,
He disappeared suddenly—none knew his lot,
His cabin did crumble to dust and decay,
But his fame will exist for many a day.

The Run and the Bridge will ever remain
To remind us of "John of the Cabin"—the same;
While the genius and skill of a great engineer
In ages to come will ever appear.[15]

According to the *Evening Star* article, a large white rock in the middle of the Potomac at the mouth of Cabin John creek was known as "John's Target," because he used it for rifle practice. With one dog he navigated the river in a crude, one-log canoe he dug out himself from a beech tree near his cabin, while another dog guarded the shoreline. Once, pranksters set fire to the woods near his cabin to smoke him out, but his stone sidewalls and sod and dirt roofing protected him. With the forest leaves burned, John's nut gathering was made easier. His past ship life was proven by the tattoos that covered his arms, legs, and entire body. "This information was obtained from some boys who stole through the bushes until they were very near John one summer day while bathing in the creek....Had he been simply a Maryland farm boy he doubtless would not have been thus decorated."[16]

It seems that John's every real or imagined movement was of interest to his community. Legend has it that he rarely went to Georgetown to trade, but

preferred places further out, such as Bladensburg, and to get there he would take a circuitous route. "In most cases he would follow trails along ravines and ridges which had been made and used by Indians many years before." When he shopped in Alexandria, he paid for his purchases with Spanish or French coins. "The report that he had a large sum of money on deposit with a firm or financial institution in Alexandria could not be verified, as the writer has been unable to find any evidence of this kind in the old records of that ancient city." One wonders how the writer verified his other tales of John. His chronicle concludes that after John disappeared and his crude abode was searched for clues about his identity, nothing was found except evidence of a rough departure, suggesting he was forced out and "dealt with in some foul manner" by his pirate associates who finally discovered his whereabouts. Thus John went to the grave in the same manner as "many of those victims of those flying marauders."[17]

Cabin John Bridge is a Washington icon. Situated over the folkloric creek, it is not surprising that the span never went by its original name, Union Arch. Its chief builder, Montgomery C. Meigs, was a staunch Union patriot (see page 143), to which the bridge bore historic testimony, for in 1862 Confederate president Jefferson Davis's name was cut from the inscription on the bridge's western abutment facing south. He had been Secretary of War before joining the Confederacy, and until the Theodore Roosevelt administration reinstated his name in 1908, at the request of the Confederate Southern Memorial Association, the inscription read:

> Washington Aqueduct
> Begun A.D. 1853. President of the U.S.,
> Franklin Pierce. Secretary of War,
> _____. Building A.D. 1861
> President of the U.S., Abraham Lincoln
> Secretary of War, Simon Cameron

As Captain D. D. Gaillard of the Army Corps of Engineers wrote in 1897, "If forgetfulness of the bare historical fact as to who was Secretary of War at the time was the object sought by the erasure, the result has been a woeful failure, for the inherent curiosity of mankind is such that the erased name is more strongly impressed upon the memory of the visitor than would have been the case had it remained untouched."[18] The inscription on the eastern abutment facing south reads:

> Union Arch
> Chief Engineer, Capt. Montgomery
> C. Meigs, U. S. Corps of Engineers
> Esto Perpetua

Brigadier General Montgomery C. Meigs (1816–1892), photographed ca. 1860–1870. Courtesy Library of Congress, Prints and Photographs Division.

Washington's first planner, Peter Charles L'Enfant, surveyed the region's major streams and rivers for a future water supply system, but the first action taken came in the early 1850s, authorizing Lieutenant (later General) Montgomery C. Meigs of the U.S. Army Corps of Engineers to undertake surveys. Of his three plans, the third was adopted to build an aqueduct system from the Potomac River just above Great Falls to the Dalecarlia reservoir. Groundbreaking began in November 1853.

Work on the Dalecarlia reservoir became a priority, as it would furnish the city with water. Thus, from 1859, several years before completion of the conduit from Great Falls, the Dalecarlia reservoir, fed by local streams, supplied water to the city. In 1863, the conduit carried Potomac water to the Dalecarlia reservoir, and following repair to several leaks, full service to the city through Cabin John Bridge was in place by 1864. During the Civil War, the bridge's wooden scaffolding was removed for fear that the Confederate army would set fire to the bridge. A dam built between the Maryland and Virginia shores just above Great Falls diverts water from the river into the mouth of the conduit:

> The water passes from the feeder, under the Chesapeake and Ohio canal, through the gatehouse and into the conduit, which is circular in cross-section, and for the greater part of its length is nine feet in diameter and composed either of rubble masonry plastered or of three rings of brick, but where the soil in which it was built was considered particularly good the inner ring of brick was omitted and the diameter was nine feet nine inches. Where the conduit passes as an unlined tunnel through rock the excavation was sufficient to contain an inscribed circle 11 feet in diameter. In 1912 and again in 1989 the conduit was lined with cement.[19]

Other modifications included the addition of a parapet wall in 1872 and steel tie-rods for support in 1912. Other reservoirs also supply Washington with water, some connected to the conduit system and others independent of it. In 1926, an additional ten-foot-diameter conduit was constructed near the Cabin John Bridge line to increase Washington's water supply. During the Second World War, Conduit Road was renamed MacArthur Boulevard to disguise the location of the city's water supply.

The adventurous walker who descends the steep southern hillside of Cabin John Bridge to look back for a view of the remarkable masonry work and famed abutment inscriptions will be well rewarded. The cut-stone arch is of granite from Quincy, Massachusetts, and the rubble arch, spandrels, and parapet walls are of Seneca sandstone. The abutments are of local, Montgomery County, gneiss.

Meigs supervised the bridge work during most of the fourteen years it took to build. The bridge is 450 feet long, 20 feet 4 inches wide, and 100 feet high, with an arch span of 220 feet. The other important bridge in Washington's aqueduct system is the Pennsylvania Avenue bridge that crosses Rock Creek near Georgetown. Two 48-inch mains form the arched ribs that support the road above.

Predominantly immigrant labor constructed Cabin John Bridge. Joseph Bobinger, from Alsace-Lorraine, began as a stone mason on the bridge, while his German wife Rosa Klein Bobinger operated a food stand from their home on government property next to the bridge. According to Edith Martin Armstrong's 1947 Cabin John history, Rosa sold "cigars, snuff, tobacco, candies, and drinks to the workmen. Later she added cakes and pies…and often served chicken dinners to the engineers."[20] By 1870, Rosa's reputation for cooking had spread, and the Bobingers bought parcels of land on the west side of the bridge and down to the Potomac; eventually they owned about one hundred acres of land on three sides of the bridge.

The Bobinger resort began with a twenty-five-room frame hotel in the style of a German tavern right next to the bridge. Later the couple added about fifteen more rooms. For years the hotel was a popular social scene for high government officials, diplomats, and leaders who "drank fine European wines from hand-etched crystal goblets." Less affluent customers "drank beer in the rathskeller."[21] The advent of the bridge—considered a wonder of the world at the time—brought visitors to the site, and the ornate, lavish hotel offered them an idyllic day. There were gardens, game rooms, bars, dance halls, fine food on Bavarian dinnerware, and access to the canal and river panoramas. A grandson of the Bobingers once said, "If it hadn't been for the bridge, there wouldn't have been a hotel…. In those days, it was, 'Let's go to Cabin John.' To start with, it would take them a while to get out there. By the time they walked through fifteen acres of park land, walked up and down the canal and watched the canal boats with the mule teams, they'd begin to get hungry. And then by the time they had two or three drinks, they were ready to go home after they finished eating. And they had a pretty ride, coming and going." At its turn of the century peak, the hotel reputedly had forty waiters, seventeen bartenders, and slot machines that produced coins "by the bucketful." One of the hotel's attractions was its orchestrion, something like a barrel organ that played music from an octagonal glass house at the back of the hotel. And there were several bandstands, from one of which John Phillip Sousa and his band played in 1900.[22]

When Joseph Bobinger died in 1881, Rosa continued the business and was the lively spirit behind the resort. At her death in 1893, her sons William and George ran the enterprise. In the early days, carriages brought patrons, and the railroad line that went out Wisconsin Avenue and Bradley Road to Great Falls had a spur to Sycamore Island, about a mile and a half from the hotel. When the trolley line from Georgetown opened around 1900, with its turnabout right at the Cabin John bridge, visitors flocked to the hotel. The sons built an enchanting cast-iron footbridge across the creek: "It had over-head horseshoes of lights all the way across the bridge, colored lights. People would get off the street car and come across the iron bridge to the hotel…. It would have been hard for a number of people to get across the aqueduct bridge, due to traffic; it's so narrow, and there were carriages and all on it."[23]

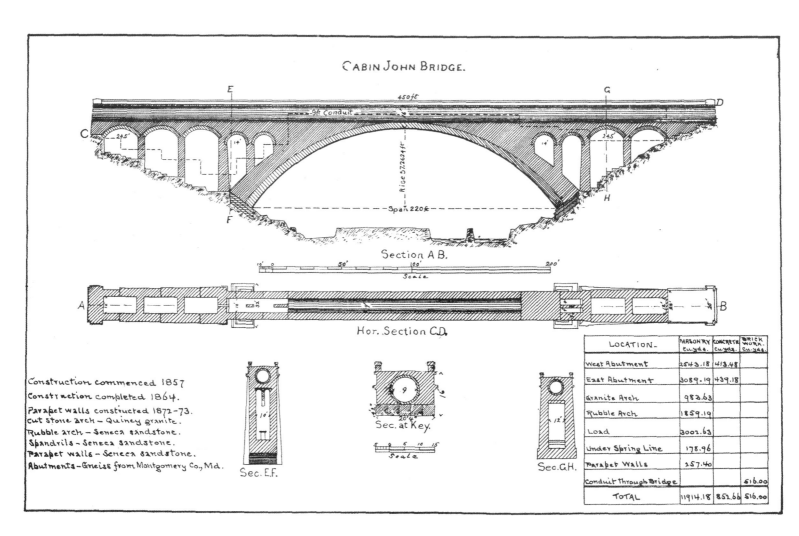

Cabin John Bridge diagram, showing its large masonry arch, National Geographic Magazine, December 1897.

Contrary to the general impression, the space between the spandril and abutment walls is not solid, but contains several arches, built, as shown in the drawing, to effect a saving in masonry. Materials were transported to the bridge by boat via the Chesapeake and Ohio canal and Cabin John creek, across which a dam was built near the canal, and the pool thus formed was connected with the latter by a lock. —D. D. Gaillard, *National Geographic Magazine,* December 1897

In 1876, the hotel installed an early Dentzel carousel, with other amusement devices following over the years. In 1900, the Bobinger sons built a full-fledged amusement park between the hotel and the creek. The rival Glen Echo amusement park opened soon after and proved more popular.

The Bobinger brothers retired from the hotel business in 1914 and rented out the building, which then closed permanently around 1925. The structure remained locked up with all its treasures until it caught fire and burned to the ground in 1931. Joseph and Rosa's grandsons said, "You almost have to think the fire was set. Nobody was in the building to cause an accidental fire....

There were so many fires in the area at that time. My wife's family's summer place burned. The old tavern at Great Falls, where the museum is, that caught fire a couple of times. Mysteriously. And a store across from Angler's Inn, that burned. Just about every vacant place burned."[24]

And so flickered out a romantic spark along the Potomac at Cabin John creek. Although a less vivacious hotel still operated when Dickinson drew Cabin John Bridge in 1918, he did not leave behind a sketch of this fabulous relic, nor of Glen Echo Park and Clara Barton's adjacent house.

The Cabin John community, rooted in this bridge, encompasses locks eight through fourteen of the C&O Canal, and lies roughly between the bridge and Persimmon Tree Road. The natural landscape now protected by the C&O Canal Historical Park forms Cabin John's front yard, and north of the community lies the vast expanse of Cabin John Regional Park, which follows the creek all the way to its source in Rockville. Carderock, a popular hiking area, is also in the vicinity, as are Glen Echo Park and the historic Clara Barton House.

After the Bobinger Hotel's fire, the federal government purchased some of the land and around 1940 developed twenty acres to house temporary defense workers at the Model Basin. One hundred prefabricated homes were built for white workers in today's Cabin John Gardens—site of the old hotel—and twenty more homes on Carver Road for African American employees. In 1955, with the war long over, the government announced that it would sell the project, and the white residents formed a cooperative to purchase their development, which remains today. Racial barriers prevented more than half the African Americans from remaining in their homes.

The canal, the river, the creek, the bridge, and a bohemian flavor continue to identify Cabin John, as does the permanency of its residents. From an annual crab fest or a canoe trip to citizen lobbies to prevent construction of malls and highways, the Cabin John community has evolved with the times to preserve its unique qualities and eclectic mix of people.[25]

The Bobinger's Cabin John Hotel, ca. 1890, with Joseph and William Kenner in the foreground. Photo by Charles J. Berner, courtesy of the Montgomery County Historical Society.

Glen Echo

Although Dickinson did not draw Glen Echo Park or the Clara Barton House, visitors to Cabin John Bridge will encounter these two historic sites, both under National Park Service administration. In 1888, enterprising twin brothers, Edwin and Edward Baltzley, bought 516 acres of land above the Potomac and formed a real estate company to sell off lots. Former president Grover Cleveland was one of the early buyers in the new development, called Glen Echo on the Potomac. The brothers' goal was a self-sufficient community with shops, post office, and a restaurant, the last of which was built immediately to boost land sales by bringing Washington's social elite to the location. The Baltzleys ensured easy accessibility by chartering the Glen Echo Railroad Company to provide trolley service to their location. From this initial real estate venture, the brothers soon invested in constructing the National Chautauqua of Glen Echo on 80 acres of their land (today's Glen Echo Park and the town). The Chautauqua movement began in the 1860s as a way to provide continuing education to workers. It also ran Sunday schools. Headquarters were in New York, and by the 1870s chapters had opened in numerous cities. Within a decade, Chautauqua summer camps flourished around the country and became the seed for Glen Echo's project in both 1890 and 1891. According to Glen Echo's historians Richard Cook and Deborah Lange, "The Baltzleys wanted the Glen Echo Chautauqua to outshine even the original Chautauqua Institute. All the buildings would be granite. Nine quarries had been opened on the property to provide material for the Chautauqua buildings and for homes and summer cottages. Plans for the second year called for building a school of fine arts, a Women's Temple, and an ornate five-story hotel."[26] The Baltzleys sought prominent teachers for the program and offered Red Cross founder Clara Barton both land and laborers to build her house within the Chautauqua grounds in exchange for her involvement. Barton became head of the Women's Executive Committee. The elaborate establishment that included an amphitheater with six thousand seats was constructed in a matter of months but enjoyed only one successful season, its opening summer of 1891.

Many of the classes focused on the causes that brought about Chautauqua, including Bible school, Greek in the New Testament, Bible for Sunday school teachers, Christian labor reform, and Christian method training for Sunday school teachers. Other classes covered more traditional subjects such as archaeology, art, astronomy, English literature, music education, music history, and physical training. In addition to courses for women in languages, music, art, and domestic sciences, the

Women's department offered progressive courses in home maintenance and business.[27]

Ironically, Glen Echo's early educational initiative did not resurface until the 1970s. Instead, to survive, the establishment became an amusement park. Rumors killed the Baltzleys' Chautauqua program at the end of its first season, when one of the teachers died of pneumonia. Word spread that he had died of malaria and that Glen Echo was rampant with the disease. The Baltzleys struggled on for another decade, with Edwin offering vaudeville in 1897, while Edward sought his fortune in Colorado gold prospecting. The Baltzleys rented out the land for an amusement park that opened in 1899, but foreclosure came in 1903. A series of new managers ran the renamed "Glen Echo Park," but until Leonard Schloss took over in 1911, the amusement park struggled to stay open. Under Schloss, it thrived for the next forty years, with a brief set-back during the forties because of another rumor, this time about a girl being bitten by a snake in the tunnel of love. "It was said that snakes were rampant in the Crystal Pool, and that the Roller Coaster had jumped its tracks killing nearly a dozen people, and that the park, because of these tragedies, had closed its gates."[28]

Once Schloss retired in 1949, decline set in. When its last manager began selling off the amusement rides, local residents mounted an effort to save first the historic Dentzel carousel and later the park itself. In 1970, the National Park Service took over administration of Glen Echo and reintroduced educational activities to the site.

Typical classes offered in the mid-1970s included ceramics, enameling, spinning, weaving, photography, drawing, painting, mixed media, fabric decorating, leather working, framing, sculpture, silk screening, drama, modern dance, social dance, music, yoga, natural foods, and ecology.[29] Federal budget cuts in the 1980s again threatened the park, and once again the citizens responded by forming Save Glen Echo Park, which raised necessary funds to maintain both programs and premises, but again for the short term, as historic preservation remains an ongoing and challenging process.

The trolley from Georgetown to Glen Echo and Cabin John provided river recreation for Washingtonians. Courtesy Library of Congress, Prints and Photographs Division.

The Baltzleys of Glen Echo rented out campgrounds with luxury tents. Photos courtesy of the Richard Cook Collection.

Clara Barton House

Clara Barton's house, built next to Glen Echo in 1891 and now a National Historic Site open to the public, was the American Red Cross headquarters from 1897 to 1904, in addition to being Barton's home until her death in 1912, at age ninety. A woman driven by the need to serve and lead in crisis situations, Barton gained renown for her Civil War battlefield work. She brought supplies, nursed the wounded, and assisted officers, earning her the nickname "Holy Angel." After the war she spent several years working both for freedmen and for families of missing soldiers. Suffering from depression throughout her life, she traveled to Europe in 1869 for recuperation and there met Dr. Louis Appia of the International Committee of the Red Cross. This organization had formed as a result of the 1864 Geneva Convention, a portion of which addressed "the treatment of wounded and sick soldiers, prisoners of war, and civilians under wartime conditions."[30] Barton gained lasting devotion to the organization when the Franco-Prussian War broke out in 1870, and she worked side by side with Red Cross volunteers in Switzerland. She wrote: "I… saw the work of Red Cross societies in the field, accomplishing in four months under this systematic organization what we failed to accomplish in four years without it—no mistakes, no needless suffering, no starving, no lack of care, no waste, no confusion, but order, plenty, cleanliness, and comfort wherever that little flag made its way, a whole continent marshaled under the banner of the Red Cross—as I saw all this, and joined and worked in it, you will not wonder that I said to myself, 'If I live to return to my country, I will try to make my people understand the Red Cross and that [Geneva] treaty.'"[31]

As a result of Barton's efforts, the Senate ratified the Treaty of Geneva in 1882, and at age sixty Barton assumed the helm of the American National Red Cross. Much of the work she accomplished during her long tenure—half of it with headquarters at Glen Echo—involved disaster relief work, including the Johnstown, Pennsylvania, flood of 1889, where 2,200 people died.[32] As an elderly, somewhat power-controlling leader at the turn of the twentieth century, Barton came under attack by younger, more professional members who went on to gain President Theodore Roosevelt's support, ultimately forcing Barton to resign her presidency at age eighty-three. Deeply hurt by this lack of respect for her lifetime achievements, Barton nevertheless continued her public service by creating, a year later, the National First Aid Society for community-aid initiatives.[33] One biography of Barton describes her as "a remarkable woman… an individual capable of firm action, strong beliefs, and an ability to see a need clearly and fulfill it. To everything she did—schoolteaching, Civil War aid, and Red Cross relief—she brought strong idealism and unfailing energy. She was truly exceptional."[34]

Washington Landmarks

WASHINGTON LANDMARKS

Cherry Blossoms

The ineffable beauty of cherry blossoms surrounding the Tidal Basin like a pale pink mist lures thousands of visitors to Washington each springtime. When Robert L. Dickinson painted this enchanting scene, the Jefferson Memorial had not yet been built, but the original Yoshino cherry trees of 1912 reflected in the water.

In 1909, Eliza Ruhamah Scidmore, who had lobbied unsuccessfully for years to plant cherry trees along the Potomac, found an enthusiastic partner in the new First Lady, Helen Herron Taft. Having lived briefly in Yokohama, Mrs. Taft immediately took up the initiative. Within days, Yoshino cherry trees had been ordered from a Pennsylvania nursery and planted. However, these trees turned out not to be the Yoshino variety and have long since disappeared. (Although numerous varieties of cherry adorn the Tidal Basin, Hain's Point, and the Washington Monument, Yoshinos predominate; they were Japan's favorite after being developed in 1870.)

While Mrs. Taft was organizing this first cherry tree planting, a famous Japanese chemist, Dr. Jokichi Takamine, heard about her efforts and offered Washington a gift from the City of Tokyo of two thousand additional trees, which Mrs. Taft accepted. Unfortunately, the donation arrived infested with insects and other diseases and had to be destroyed. Dr. Takamine arranged for a second, even larger tree shipment, and this one arrived without any setbacks on March 26, 1912. The very next day, Mrs. Taft and the Japanese ambassador's wife, Viscountess Chinda, planted the first two Yoshino trees at the Tidal Basin, near Independence Avenue, SW, where they stand to this day, marked by a plaque. Mrs. Taft's planting ceremony of one hundred years ago, which enhanced the city's beauty and unique identity, was also the starting point for today's popular Cherry Blossom Festival.

Besides creating a sublime atmosphere, Washington's cherry blossoms symbolize the longstanding friendship between the capital city and Japan. The trees came to Washington as a gift from the City of Tokyo, and more gifts followed over the years, including a three-hundred-year-old stone lantern, a Japanese pagoda, and 3,800 additional Yoshino trees in 1965.

The exchange has been reciprocal, for when the Japanese grove that had fathered Washington's trees fell into decline after World War II, the National Park Service sent budwood from the Tidal Basin trees to help regenerate the ancestral grove. Since the new millennium, some four hundred trees have been propagated from the remaining 1912 trees to preserve the original lineage.[1]

Every year, when the trees bloom in late March to early April, Washington goes all out to celebrate its own rite of spring, which the annual festival enriches through public programming. Cherry blossoms are as synonymous with Washington as the White House, and so Dickinson's legacy from 1918 becomes all the more precious.

I bicycled along the embankment alone, through a world embowered, under canopied masses of white bloom. The scene was magical, as if reality had given way to an illusory kingdom of flower and light, the light shimmering and ghostlike in its reflection from the masses of bloom overhead. They seemed a distillation of light without weight or substance. The landscape was arrayed as if the earth were having its own mystic wedding festival, all in white close up, nacreous white in the distance, across the mirror of still water. It was silent and motionless, like a vision too insubstantial to last beyond the moment. The reality above seemed no less a wonderful illusion than its reflection in the water below. —Louis J. Halle, *Spring in Washington, 1947*

Washington in April 1918,
Japanese cherries.

The Japanese cherries by the Tide Pool
and the Lincoln Memorial, April 3, 1918.

Smithsonian

The Smithsonian Institution is unique in the world. Five of its art, history, and science museums line the National Mall, and several others are within walking distance. Called "the nation's attic" by Mark Twain, most of the Smithsonian's extensive exhibitions and public programming—including the annual Folklife Festival—are free. So many visitors flock to the Smithsonian museums that the Mall—the vast greenway between the Capitol and the Washington Monument— really feels like the American people's space.

The Smithsonian's collections and research activities began in about 1838, following the settlement of British scientist John Smithson's will, which bequeathed $508,000 to the young United States "to found in Washington under the name of the Smithsonian Institution, an establishment for the increase and diffusion of knowledge among men."[2] In 1838, the gift reached the United States government, and in 1846 Congress passed an act for the creation of an appropriate research institution and museum and also the new facility's programs. The Smithsonian's "Castle" building, designed by James Renwick, was completed in 1855.

It is believed that personal reasons prompted Smithson's gift. His often-quoted line, "My name shall live in the memory of man when the titles of the Northumberland and the Percys are extinct and forgotten," has never been verified through an original document, and some older Washington guidebooks have overemphasized his illegitimate status as motivation for the bequest. The bequest's language includes Enlightenment idealism, such as references to faith in the value of research and knowledge to improve human conditions.[3] When Smithson died in 1826, his will stated that if his nephew died without heirs, then his personal fortune would go to the United States for founding the Smithsonian Institution.

From the time of its inception, the Smithsonian steadily grew, expanding its collections, its research, and its real estate holdings. Since 1858, it has received an annual appropriation from Congress. The Smithsonian's first secretary, Joseph Henry, focused on scientific research, but his successor, Spencer Fullerton Baird, was intent on developing a national museum, and following the 1876 Centennial Exposition "convinced most exhibitors to donate their displays to the Smithsonian."[4] Baird also successfully lobbied to build the National Museum Building, today's Arts and Industries building. Under his stewardship the Smithsonian opened the Bureau of American Ethnology, whose founding director was explorer John Wesley Powell (1834–1902). Successive leaders added more programs and museums. More recently, the institution's collections and research activities have faced serious financial challenges, affecting its early spirit of creative activity. Upgrading and maintaining the historic buildings alone exceeds the institution's annual appropriation. Luckily, the redbrick Arts and Industries building designed by Adolf Cluss in 1879 is being restored.

Smithsonian tower and the Monument, April 1918.

Smithsonian Tower
and the Monument
April — 59·8

WITH THE RAMBLER

If you are passing across the front of the Smithsonian Institution at midnight and hear strange cries coming from the Byzantine, Norman or rounded Gothic towers, buttresses, battlements, groined arches and cornices, keep your nerve. The moon may be floating through the southern sky. Now it will be hidden under dense cloud masses, and then it will burst through the black mist and cast its silver sheen over the heavens and the earth. Against all this, the long red sandstone buildings, dark but for a watchman's lamp in the central vestibule, will be submitted. It looks gloomy and lonesome. One almost feels the damp and stagnant vapor that would rise from the moat around it, if a moat were there. One can almost hear the clank of armor, as a sentinel in scale, or plate, or steel link chain strides the battlements. It is very lonesome, and if there were graves around it would be the best place in the city for ghosts. Perhaps perturbed spirits do stalk there. The cries, now sharp, now muffled, now seeming the agony of strangulation, come to your ears from those grim and towering walls. It sounds like tragedy.

You can reassure yourself that you are not in the depths of a haunted forest and before some dismal medieval castle by looking northward to catch the glitter of the lights in the post office tower or by listening to the purr and soft ripple of the fountain not far removed from the northwest corner of the building.

The sounds that have stopped you, and it may be, chilled you, come from—not mortals—but from bats. There are many of these aberrant insectivorae or flying mammals, family gallopithecidae, order of chiroptern, in the shadowy nooks of the Smithsonian building.

Satisfied that no harm is near, you fall to thinking of James Smithson's bequest of 1826; of James Renwick, the designer of this building, the first of its style not ecclesiastic, to be reared in the United States; your glance goes up to the top of the tallest tower 140 feet above the asphalt, all strewn with dead leaves, and your mind goes back to the time when President Polk and his cabinet and hundreds of proud men, now dust, attended the corner stone laying in 1847; to the time when the building was finished in 1856, and to the time of the great fire in 1865, when irreparable losses were sustained—such as may be again sustained by the clumsy habit of the government in packing priceless things in flimsy buildings. —The Rambler, *Evening Star,* December 8, 1912

* * *

In the Smithsonian grounds about fifty feet north from and at the back of the bronze statue of Joseph Henry, off the northwest corner of the Smithsonian building, is a drinking fountain that purrs all summer, but which is silent now. In the body of the iron work are the heads of two creatures, probably sea serpents, and from the mouths of these the water flows. It is one of the usual old-style park drinking fountains and combination lamp posts, and at night this fountain stands as a beacon at a crossroads in the Smithsonian grounds. It is noted here that the heads may be those of sea serpents. They may also be the heads of big eels or water moccasins, but they probably are not. The fountain architects must have had a wide knowledge of the fauna of mythology.—The Rambler, *Evening Star,* January 26, 1913

Note: In 1965 the Henry statue was moved and rotated to face the Mall.

Franklin Park, also Franklin Square

During his Washington stay, Robert L. Dickinson lived at 1424 K Street, at Franklin Park, a lovely tree-filled slope bounded by K, I, Thirteenth, and Fourteenth Streets, NW. It was considered a posh neighborhood in its heydey, with handsome architecture that included Adolf Cluss's Franklin Terrace row houses (1875) and his celebrated Franklin School (1868, still standing). Only a few blocks from the White House, the park was close to downtown's liveliest scene of restaurants, theaters, and hotels. Of Washington's several downtown parks, Franklin's undulating, sylvan topography offers the greatest landscape potential. Unfortunately, the area's dramatic decline from the Depression years on through the 1968 riots devastated the park and connected it to the city's red-light district. More recently, the downtown commercial real estate boom and efforts by Casey Trees have improved the park's neglect.

Early in the capital city's history, Franklin Park's location gained notice because of its several natural springs in close proximity to the White House. In 1832, Congress appropriated funds to purchase "City Square 249," apparently influencing the park's first name, Fountain Square. The 4.8-acre parcel was intended for building lots and not a park, though the government's motive for the purchase was to supply water to the White House, the Treasury, and the State, War, and Navy Building (today's Old Executive Office Building). Eventually named for Benjamin Franklin, the square's famous Cluss buildings also incorporated this name—Franklin School and Franklin Terrace row houses.

During the Civil War, Union troops from New York lived in barracks in the park, and Secretary of War Edwin M. Stanton resided at 1323 K Street, on the square's north side. It was during the postwar surge in city improvements that the fashionable residential community sprang up around the square. The park gained a fountain in the early 1870s and gas lamps in the 1880s. In 1914, the bronze statue of commodore John Barry by John J. Boyle was erected in the park, commemorating an Irish immigrant who became a Revolutionary War hero when he was the first to capture a British ship.[5]

During the New Deal, the Works Progress Administration installed today's central fountain, replacing the original one seen in Dickinson's idyllic drawing.

Franklin Park, a magnolia in March, Washington, DC.

Franklin Park
a magnolia
in March
Washington D.C.

Franklin Park, Washington, DC.

Dickinson's sketch from his residence at Franklin Park. Papers of Robert Latou Dickinson, 1883–1950 [B MS c72], Boston Medical Library in the Francis A. Countway Library of Medicine.

Justice Department

When Robert L. Dickinson sketched this shrouded view of the Denrike building at the corner of Vermont Avenue and K Street, NW, it housed Justice Department offices, including their "secret service," a detective division not affiliated with the Treasury Department's famous Secret Service. Created in 1908 as the Bureau of Investigation, the Justice Department's secret service grew over the years and in 1935 was renamed the Federal Bureau of Investigation (FBI). Dickinson could see the Denrike building from his residence at Fourteenth and K Streets, NW.

From its inception in 1789 as the Office of the Attorney General, when it was a one-man, part-time, and parsimoniously paid job, the Justice Department roved without a permanent home until 1934, when it gained its own building on Pennsylvania Avenue between Ninth and Tenth Streets, NW, one that also housed the FBI until the 1970s. Ulysses S. Grant signed a bill establishing the Department of Justice in 1870, and today this agency is "the largest law firm in the country," with more than fourteen hundred offices in the United States and abroad. Under the department's jurisdiction fall the FBI, the United States Marshals Service, the Federal Bureau of Prisons, the Drug Enforcement Administration, and other offices. Listed below are some of the locations of the formerly roving Justice Department.

The Denrike building at the corner of Vermont Avenue and K Street. Courtesy the FBI.

1822   a room on the second floor of the old War Building.

1839   the second floor of the Treasury Building, where the office remained for sixteen years.

1855   a yellow brick building on the southeast corner of Fifteenth and F Streets, NW, for six years.

1861   a suite of rooms on the first floor of the Treasury Building's south wing for ten years; staff was scattered in various locations in this period, leading to a Department of Justice in every state. One of the assistant attorney generals and the solicitor general were housed in the Hooe Iron building on F Street near Fourteenth Street, NW.

1871   the Freedman's Savings Bank building on Pennsylvania Avenue, NW, for ten years; when the lease expired in 1882, Congress appropriated funds to purchase the building, and for the first time the department had its own, though short-lived, home.

1899   the Palmer House, later the Baltic Hotel, at 1435 K Street, NW, with other offices dispersed in a half-dozen or more buildings. Justice vacated this building in 1917.

1917   Denrike building at the corner of Vermont Avenue and K Street, NW, housed the Bureau of Investigation—Dickinson's "secret service"— until 1934.[6]

Our view, Secret Service,
Dept. Justice, April 1918.

WASHINGTON
St. John's Church The whitehouse
the Monument & the Potomac   Dickinson 1918

St. John's Church, Lafayette Square

St. John's, "The Church of the Presidents," situated across Lafayette Square from the White House, was completed in 1816 according to Benjamin Henry Latrobe's design. The famous architect reportedly said, "I have completed a church that has made many Washingtonians religious who had not been religious before."

Every president since James Madison has attended services at the church, either as a member or on special occasions. Over its long history, several renovations have taken place, including its belfry addition in the early 1820s and the stained glass windows by Madame Veuve Lorin, a curator at Chartres Cathedral, in 1833.[7]

Dickinson made several drawings of St. John's Church and likely attended some services there, not only because he was an Episcopalian, but also because the church was historic, picturesque, and within blocks of his residence; church records, however, do not list him as a guest member.

St. John's Church, the White House, the Monument, and the Potomac, 1918.

Courtesy Papers of Robert Latou Dickinson, 1883–1950 [B MS c72], Boston Medical Library in the Francis A. Countway Library of Medicine.

A winter's evening, St. John's,
the Monument, the White
House, December 1917.

Georgetown

Georgetown, long a seaport hub before joining the Federal District in 1871, was separated from Washington proper by Rock Creek, a beautiful, rocky stream that is barely visible today from the Rock Creek Parkway, a winding four-lane road that follows the streambed. Long ago, Rock Creek's mouth at the Potomac River formed a basin terminus for Georgetown's water-generated commerce. As a result, the area's sloping embankments had the appearance of a dumpsite. Today, these same hillsides have been landscaped and in springtime are covered with acres of daffodils. A bike path follows the graceful roadway, adding to the feel of a continuous sylvan space stretching from Washington's Mall all the way to Maryland's portion of Rock Creek Park.

The Georgetown neighborhood has no rival in Washington for its quaint, historic beauty and landscape allures. The town descends steeply toward the Potomac in an inviting array of redbrick and clapboard townhouses that from the opposite shore at night glitter romantically. Georgetown's tree-lined streets, running more or less in grid fashion on either side of Wisconsin Avenue, retain their historic flavor. Some even retain their cobblestones, and most are redolent of flowering gardens. The neighborhood—home to high society and the political elite for more than two centuries—hosts annual house and garden tours. Along the brick sidewalks, a number of historic houses remain, the most famous being Tudor Place, at 1644 Thirty-first Street, NW. This neoclassical house was built in 1816 by Thomas Peter, son of Georgetown's first mayor, who married Martha Parke Custis, one of Martha Washington's granddaughters. The house stayed in the family until the 1980s and is now a National Historic Landmark with a museum and garden open to the public. Redbrick Dumbarton Oaks, at 1703 Thirty-second Street, NW, is another architectural treasure and houses a Byzantine collection and library owned by Harvard University. Architect Philip Johnson designed the museum portion. A splendid garden is open to the public and abounds with visitors in the spring. Georgetown's Oak Hill Cemetery dates to 1849 and has been called "a jewel of a park…set on a wooded hillside above a rushing stream. Vaults and obelisks, with carved angels hovering and Greek temples glimpsed, all gently infiltrated by winding paths beneath elemental oaks through glorious landscape."[8] Architect James Renwick designed the chapel and the iron enclosure.

Francis Scott Key was one of the many notable people who have lived in Georgetown. His M Street house was demolished in 1947, to build the Whitehurst Freeway. As a young lawyer in 1814, Key attempted to free his uncle, Dr. William Beane, from capture by the British Fleet, but ended up imprisoned himself. From a British flagship he witnessed the bombardment of Fort McHenry and wrote the "Star-Spangled Banner."

Georgetown (called Town of George and George Town in its early years) was a Native American village named Tohoga, when documented by the British fur trader Henry Fleet in 1632. For the rest of the seventeenth century, immigrant

Georgetown from above the first quarry on the Potomac.

In Dickinson's drawing the spires of Georgetown University, a familiar landmark to local residents, pierce the sky. In the background, Aqueduct Bridge (replaced by Key Bridge in 1923) crosses the placid Potomac River. On the Arlington shore, evidence of a quarry with rudimentary dwellings documents a way of life along the Potomac that has left almost no other trace. The black rectangle on the Aqueduct Bridge could be the railroad. The Rambler article on Georgetown refers to "the track of a steam railroad" that runs along Water Street, referring to the Georgetown Branch of the B&O.

settlers moved into the area, many of them Scottish. In 1703, Ninian Beall obtained a land grant from the Province of Maryland, a British colony, for 795 acres of land, which he named Rock of Dunbarton, after a site in Scotland. The Beall family's land holdings grew, and two generations later, George Beall partnered with another large landholder, George Gordon, to open a tobacco inspection house at the port. In 1751, the Maryland Assembly established Georgetown on 60 acres of land purchased from Beall and Gordon, and Georgetown may have been named for these two Georges. For many years, the town thrived as a tobacco port, and in 1789 became officially chartered, with the prominent tobacco merchant, Robert Peter, becoming mayor. Almost a century later, in 1871, Georgetown was incorporated into the Federal District, and in 1895 it was required to change its street names to conform to the Washington grid plan of lettered and numbered streets.[9]

Georgetown has a long frontier-town history that includes both economic prosperity and severe depression. As an early port town for tobacco, it had to compete with Alexandria and later with Washington City, and eventually, in the early 1800s, it declined, partly because the river silted up preventing reliable trade access. By mid-century, however, development of the C&O Canal brought new commercial opportunities in coal and flour trade, and until the end of the nineteenth century Georgetown's waterfront was a lively manufacturing scene that included mills, iron foundries, and lime kilns. It also thrived as a shopping district and growing residential community with many civic activities, including clubs and societies for hobbies and interests. Georgetown College, founded in 1789, was considered "the new capital's only center of intellectual life."[10]

Preserving historic Georgetown and its irreplaceable shoreline, which includes the C&O Canal towpath and Capital Crescent Trail, takes extraordinary community and legislative effort. Many environmental and outdoors groups work hard to make sure waterfront projects do not affect trails, parkland, and natural habitats. One citizen group, the Coalition for the Capital Crescent Trail (CCCT), succeeded in the late 1980s in converting the

WITH THE RAMBLER

Region of Steps

Attention has been called by the Rambler to the steep streets of Georgetown, and also to some of those streets the grade of which is only overcome by the use of steps. A multitude of people climb up and down the steep stone stairway of 36th street from N street into the car shed off M street. It is an important transfer point, and people are toiling on these stairs every hour in the day. There are also stairs on 33d and 34th streets, that lead down from M street to the towpath of the Chesapeake and Ohio canal, and more steps that lead down to Water street.

As you enter upon the Aqueduct bridge you may see persons going up and down a flight of steps on the east side of the bridge. They lead from the first span of the bridge—the span which crosses the canal and Water street—down to the west bank of the canal. These are much used steps. When you reach the level of the canal you will see that Georgetown is still far below. A gray stone wall rises from the level of Water street to the level of the canal, and across the face of this wall are two flights of wooden steps, painted this season a pale green color. They are as steep as the average inclination of a ladder, but the broad tread and the handrails aid persons in descending and ascending.

Water street is lined with warehouses, wharves and boat club houses, and the track of a steam rail-road runs along the middle of the granite block and cobblestone pavement. The street and the railroad pass through a wide and graceful stone arch beneath the bridge. It is a quiet neighborhood except during the work hours of week days, when strings of people may be seen using the steep stairways.

Looking up from Water street at this point, the scene is filled with iron girders, beams, braces, and steps. —The Rambler, *Evening Star*, November 16, 1913

B&O's Georgetown Branch rail line into a paved and scenic path for bikers, joggers, walkers, and other fresh-air seekers. The eleven-mile coal-carrying branch operated from 1889 to 1985. When it closed, various interest groups immediately competed to purchase the corridor from the CSX Corporation (a railroad conglomerate) for their own projects, such as a new freight line, a scenic rail line, and a mass transit plan. The CCCT lobbied for the wooded, multiuse trail that gives pleasure to so many residents and visitors today. Washington philanthropist Kingdon Gould Jr. played a key role in preserving the 3.6 miles of rail line that lie within the District of Columbia for ultimate inclusion in the C&O Canal National Historical Park. At the critical moment, he put up the $10 million needed to purchase that section of the line, earning him renown as "savior of the trail." Simultaneously, the National Park Service contracted with Gould to buy the right of way within one year, so that the trail now operates under the Park Service's stewardship. The CCCT's lobbying efforts also led to Montgomery County purchasing the trail's Maryland portion for inclusion in the county system, ensuring an uninterrupted 10-mile trail from Silver Spring to Georgetown.

Taft Bridge

The soaring and graceful Taft Bridge carries Connecticut Avenue across Rock Creek gorge at a height of 125 feet above the valley. Designed by George S. Morison, the bridge was under construction from 1897 to 1907. Originally named the Connecticut Avenue Bridge, it soon acquired the nickname the Million Dollar Bridge because of its high cost—some $846,000. In 1931, the bridge was renamed for President William Howard Taft, who had lived nearby and made it part of his regular exercise route. Taft was president from 1909 to 1913 and chief justice from 1921 to 1930, the year of his death.

Among Washington's early, large bridges, the Taft stood as a landmark in concrete construction. Two wooden creek crossings preceded it, followed by an iron truss deck structure (1888), which became obsolete by the late 1890s. Concrete lions sculpted by Roland Hinton Perry more than one hundred years ago stood at each end of the bridge. When a restoration attempt in the 1990s proved impossible owing to their deterioration, artist Reinaldo López-Carrizo cast new lions from the originals, and these were installed in 2000.

Dickinson's landscape drawings during the Washington war effort portray romantic, often idyllic scenes. In his second drawing of the Taft Bridge, however, the backdrop of World War I makes an appearance. In April 1918, the government organized a Liberty Bonds drive, with April 26 declared a Liberty Loan Day holiday. To promote sales, the 1916 tank Britannia came to town as "a souvenir of British courage." The *Evening Star* described the tank climbing the hills and crushing trees in its path near the Connecticut Avenue bridge with 60,000 onlookers, as illustrated in Dickinson's picture. On close inspection of the drawing, an airplane can be seen in the top center. The newspaper also reported that an Italian airplane circled overhead, with the airmen waving to the crowd. The headline for the story was "Tank and Airplane in Day of Thrills."[11]

*Taft Bridge (formerly the
Connecticut Avenue Bridge).*

Sixty-thousand people look on from the bridge.
The tank beats down trees and climbs muddy
banks, April 1918. The boy falls into the river.

Spring in Rock Creek Park.

Rock Creek Park

Washingtonians treasure Rock Creek Park—it is a beautiful, natural wilderness in the middle of the city. Many streets run through it, allowing residents to feel personally connected to its wooded refuge. In 1918, Frederick Law Olmsted Jr. wrote a report for its maintenance, and today the National Park Service oversees its preservation, which is a continuous challenge, as the park's 1,700 hundred acres occupy prime real estate in the nation's capital. Many recreational users of the park hope that some day its principal roads—never intended for today's commuter traffic—will close at least part of the day so that the park can be a true retreat with greater protection of its threatened environment.

In 1890, Congress passed the Rock Creek Park bill, authorizing specified land to be "perpetually dedicated and set apart for the benefit and enjoyment of the people of the United States." This initiative occurred during the era of creating city and national parks, a movement spearheaded by the father of landscape architecture in America, Frederick Law Olmsted (1822–1903). His son, FLO Jr., became an influential member of the 1901 Senate Park Commission responsible for Washington's "beautification," or redesign in the spirit of Peter Charles L'Enfant's tradition. FLO Jr. also helped to create the Commission of Fine Arts in 1910, to implement the Senate Park Commission's plan. A few years later he was asked to study Rock Creek Park, and his 1918 report came to Dickinson's attention. Perhaps coincidentally, this is the only section of Dickinson's Walk Book manuscript that is hastily sketched out.[12] In it he wrote:

> Rock Creek Park is a very personal park. You, yourself, really discovered it. Even though someone may have led you to it. The very name flashes pictures on your screen. One such flash is the autumn woods in full color in the late afternoon when, happily lost on a vanishing trail, on a down-dropping ridge, you lingered dreaming, to listen to the murmuring river beneath, and the dust overtook you and the light failed....
>
> The next picture to leap into color is that of the hot noon when, tired by clambering over one hillside after another, you stepped abruptly out of dim forest tangle on to the brilliant still green meadow, with the willows trailing in the mirror above the dam. That was the first day you lunched at the Mill....
>
> Or, last of all, that morning in Springtime, when gazing through the delicate mist, up at the two bridges hung high in the sky, on a turn in the roadway, there, on a bench in the banked blooming laurel—all of a sudden—Herself. It is a very personal Park.[13]

Dickinson's title for his Rock Creek Park drawing, which includes "STD and me," suggests that the "Herself" in this passage refers to his wife, Sarah Truslow Dickinson (STD).

Part of the other picnic, Rock Creek Park, May 18, 1918, STD and me.

St. Paul's Church

Located next to the Soldiers' Home (Armed Forces Retirement Home) in Brookland, Northeast Washington, St. Paul's Episcopal Church, also called Rock Creek Church, is the oldest and the only Georgian colonial church in Washington. Its redbrick exterior stands nobly on an incline, surrounded by rolling green space that includes the Rock Creek Cemetery, resting place of many contributors to local and national history, such as Henry and Marian Adams, Alexander "Boss" Shepherd, Upton Sinclair, and Gilbert Grosvenor.

In 1712, Reverend John Fraiser held regular services for the neighborhood, and in 1719 one of his parishioners, Colonel John Bradford, donated 100 acres of land for the present-day church. The original church was replaced in 1775, remodeled in 1868, and then rebuilt in 1921, following a devastating fire. Dickinson's drawing of St. Paul's documents not only the church before it burned down but also the "glebe oak" at the church entrance, felled in the 1980s after surviving five hundred years on the property. In 2004, the church interior underwent complete renovation.

One of the most moving statues in the world can be visited in Rock Creek Cemetery—the Adams Memorial, commonly known as Grief. Henry Adams (1838–1918) commissioned sculptor Augustus Saint-Gaudens (1848–1907) to create a monument marking the grave of his wife, Marian Hooper Adams, who fell into a depression after her father's death and commited suicide by poisoning herself with the potassium cyanide she used for developing photographs.

Grief-stricken, Adams traveled through Japan, read Buddhist philosophy, and returned to Washington with ideas for a memorial to his wife. He asked Saint-Gaudens not for her portrait or likeness, but for a figure that represented "the acceptance, intellectually, of the inevitable." The artist's androgynous bronze sculpture embodied the "ambiguity many Westerners admired in Asian religion and philosophy." Stanford White designed the statue's granite bench and backdrop. Adams's close friend John Hay described the work as "indescribably noble and imposing. Infinite wisdom; a past without beginning and a future without end; a repose, after limitless experience; a peace, to which nothing matters—all embodied in this austere and beautiful face and form." Adams spent many solitary hours contemplating the sculpture and wrote in third person about his own response to it:

> He was apt to stop there often to see what the figure had to tell him that was new; but, in all that it had to say, he never once thought of questioning what it meant. He supposed its meaning to be the one commonplace about it—the oldest idea known to human thought. He knew that if he asked an Asiatic its meaning, not a man, woman, or child from Cairo to Kamtchatka would have needed more than a glance to reply. From the Egyptian Sphinx to the Kamakura Daibuts; from Prometheus to Christ; from Michael Angelo to Shelley, art had wrought on this eternal figure almost as though it had nothing else to say.[14]

St. Gaudens's statue known as Grief. Photo by Ernie Brooks, © 2004, Rock Creek Images.

Dickinson pasted a photograph of *Grief* into his album of drawings.

ST. PAVLS CHURCH 1712 : ROCK CREEK CEMETERY .
close to the Henry Adams Monument

St. Paul's Church, 1712, Rock Creek Cemetery,
close to the Henry Adams Monument.

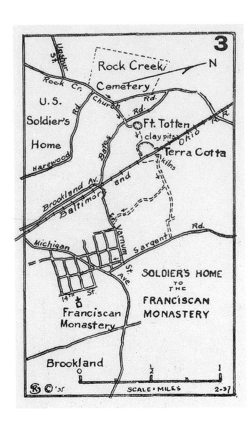

Soldiers Home to the Franciscan Monastery. **Robert Shosteck,** *Guide to Trails around Washington.* © **Robert Shosteck, 1937.**

The Soldiers' Home

For many Washingtonians the name "Soldiers' Home" conjures up an immediate response of curiosity, for little is readily known about the large green space in Northwest Washington's farthest reach, next to Catholic University and the Rock Creek Cemetery. Officially renamed the Armed Forces Retirement Home (AFRH), and referred to as "the campus," this hilly and historically intriguing enclave of Washington has been rarely visited by tourists or locals. Private sector development in the home's southwest corner, including parks and paths for public use, will change this seclusion. Matthew Pinsker's book *Lincoln's Sanctuary: Abraham Lincoln and the Soldiers' Home* (2003) brought attention to the home and President Lincoln's use of the Gothic Revival–style cottage on the premises. In 2000, the cottage was designated a National Monument, and the National Trust for Historic Preservation restored it as a learning center on Lincoln and his presidency. Thus, a fresh lease on life that integrates the public and the neighborhood has transformed the campus's declining state.[15]

From the late nineteenth century or before, Washingtonians had strolled the home's parklike grounds, and a streetcar from downtown along Seventh Street (Georgia Avenue) made the neighborhood accessible. After Washington's riots in the 1960s, however, the home's gates closed to the public for security reasons.

The Soldiers' Home has a fascinating, 150-year history, with the Civil War years noteworthy for Lincoln's use of the cottage as a "summer White House." Originally built for George W. Riggs in 1842, the house was purchased by the Military Asylum's Board of Commissioners in 1851 and later named Anderson Cottage after Major Robert Anderson, who lobbied hard for a military retirement home. His partners in this decades-long campaign were Jefferson Davis and General Winfield Scott. Once their goal was achieved, pressure to keep the home financially solvent became an ongoing challenge for the board. Nevertheless, the Riggs farm purchase was an excellent choice in property, perhaps even too much so, according to Paul Goode, one the home's historians from the 1950s:

> In the overall picture, the choice finally made was a good one…because during the past hundred years there have been many attempts to secure part or all of the land; and these attempts, actuated by motives ranging from the frankly predatory to those thinly disguised as more worthy, have been made by types ranging from members of the real estate business and the Bureau of the Budget to governmental agencies of Cabinet rank. The fact that the land was not bought by appropriated funds, but paid for by the enlisted men of the Army, has always been conveniently overlooked.[16]

HOSPITAL OF
SOLDIERS HOME
FROM THE SCOTT STATUE   CAPITOL   POTOMAC   MONUMENT

 From The Scott statue

Hospital of Soldiers' Home
from the Scott statue.

Lincoln Cottage, ca. 1863. Courtesy of The Lincoln Museum, Fort Wayne, Indiana (no. 3993).

The cottage became Lincoln's summer and fall residence, for its breezy hilltop location offered cooler weather and healthier conditions than the Potomac bog around the White House three miles away. Among the highlights of Lincoln's occupancy, three stories are often told. First, he probably drafted his emancipation policy at the cottage. Second, on an evening in August 1864, when the president was riding his horse home from the White House, an assassin shot at him. But galloping hard, Lincoln made it safely to Soldiers' Home. The guard on duty had heard the shot and noticed the president's hat was not on his head. He and another guard went out to search the area and found Lincoln's stovepipe hat with a bullet hole through the crown.[17] Third, Lincoln was living at the Soldiers' Home when the Civil War's Battle of Fort Stevens broke out (see page 149). During the heat of cross-fire, he climbed a parapet to watch the action. When a surgeon standing next to him was hit, General Horatio Wright told the president to get down. However, a more popular version of the story says that Captain Oliver Wendell Holmes, then aide to General Wright, told the president, "Get down, you damn fool, before you get shot!" Pinsker's recent research supports the Horatio Wright version.[18]

Other presidents also made a summer residence of the Soldiers' Home, including James Buchanan, Rutherford B. Hayes, and Chester Arthur. But the role of the home as a presidential retreat was a small part of its true mission. The young United States had an acute need for a "soldiers' asylum" in the early nineteenth century. Between the years 1790 and 1860, the country had fought in twenty-three wars. Severe hardship defined the life of the typical soldier, and many lost limbs, suffered disease, and ended up beggars on the streets. Pensions amounted to about five dollars a month until 1851, when they were raised to eight dollars. Thus the need was real for establishing an army retirement home.[19]

Over it's long history, the Soldiers' Home has offered care for aging and disabled military personnel. First it served the regular army; then, after World War II, it included the Air Force and was renamed the U.S. Soldiers' and Airmen's Home. In 1991, Congress folded Gulfport's Naval Home into the AFRH agency; in 2002, new legislation opened the home to the entire armed forces.[20] Until 1859, the home was called the Military Asylum (changed in 1859 to the Soldiers' Home), and for many more years its members were called inmates, common terminology of the day. As Goode writes in his history, "The story of the Soldiers' Home is an honorable one for it was the first effort to care for those who had given the country much; in many cases, a country not of their birth."[21] The home's early, strict military system and uniforms eased over time, and today it appears much like other retirement homes, except that its residents are 90 percent male; this represents a reversal of the typical gender ratio in retirement communities.

From the 1830s, the government had consistently voted down bills to fund a direly needed "Army Asylum," so that one of its principal proponents, General Winfield Scott, took matters into his own hands. During the Mexican War (1846–1848), he had gained a ransom of about $150,000 in exchange for not pillaging Mexico City. In those days of poor pay for enlisted men, soldiers were allowed to loot conquered cities. For instance, during the Civil War, Frederick, Maryland, paid the Confederate Lieutenant General Jubal A. Early $200,000 so that he would not burn the town. General Scott made sure $100,000 of his Mexican ransom went to founding the Soldiers' Home. It was governed by a Board of Commissioners, an appointed governor, deputy governor, surgeon, and secretary-treasurer. Over the century and a half since its opening, the home's administrative roles have changed. New legislation in 2002 established an appointed chief operative officer (COO), who heads the AFRH and reports to the Secretary of Defense. Each facility within the establishment has its own director, who reports to the COO. The home's demographics have also changed. In the early years, a majority of residents were from recent immigrant families, but by 1913, American residents outnumbered the foreign-born.[22]

Despite the need for a retirement home for disabled soldiers, the spacious Soldiers' Home, with its historic buildings, has always been subject to scrutiny, and its opponents over the decades have tried to close it, reduce its land holdings, or otherwise arrest its growth or improvements, often claiming that it is a burden to the federal government and a misuse of taxpayer money. Yet, the Soldiers' Home has maintained its financial independence. Its funding comes from several sources, including an automatic paycheck deduction from military personnel. The home also applies to Congress each year for use of its own trust fund investments. When the Soldiers' Home was founded, the payroll deduction for enlisted men was two and one-half cents. Today it is fifty cents. The current approximate breakdown for generating the AFRH's income consists of monthly payroll deductions, resident fees, fines and forfeitures, and sales or leases.

By the turn of the twenty-first century, some of the home's unique buildings, such as Stanley Hall and the Grant Building, were largely unusable for their intended purpose, and the AFRH has looked for creative ways to save them, such as leasing them to other groups or organizations. Such innovations complement the home's master plan for private sector development of 77 acres in the southeast section. In 2005, Catholic University purchased 49 acres of land adjacent to its southeast border.[23]

For years the home's population was small but over its first century grew to twenty-five hundred members, and now numbers about one thousand. A feeling of history permeates the old buildings. The hilltop landscape is still beautiful with manicured lawns, proud governors' mansions built of New York marble, and architectural specimens such as the Grant Building that dates from the turn of the twentieth century and the Sherman Building (originally the Scott Dormitory), with a clock tower that served as a signal post during the Civil War. It is said that the tower's spire on the southwest corner is taller than the others, for it was raised when the Washington Monument was built, to retain its distinction as the highest point in Washington. Several miles of roadway wind through the premises as if through a colonial settlement. The Rose Chapel from 1870 is built of red Seneca sandstone and stands in contrast to the newer, more functional buildings.

The home, once encompassing about 500 acres, has been whittled down to 272 acres to widen North Capitol Street and to build the Washington Hospital complex, for which the home received little or no compensation. Fortunately the retirees' nine-hole golf course survived these real estate losses. Providing enough leisure activities for residents was an early challenge for the home, spurring the addition of a theater, a library, an art studio, and a golf course. Movies, cards, chess, and billiards were other early and popular activities. One of the land encroachment stories affecting the Soldiers' Home involves the golf course, for under holes two and three lies a district reservoir. As Goode wryly commented in his history: "The proposal to establish the reservoir was first made in 1937, with the usual preamble that in all Washington only the land of the Soldiers' Home was suitable for that purpose."[24] The trade-off for the home was that it would receive free water forever, an agreement that continues to be upheld.

Across Harewood Street along the home's northern boundary is the 16-acre Soldiers' Home National Cemetery (maintained by Arlington National Cemetery), where residents are buried to this day. This site is open to the public and abuts the property of Rock Creek Cemetery, the location of St. Paul's church. Washington is fortunate to have such a fascinating military retirement home among its historic properties. Through a century and a half of struggles, the home continues to survive, and protecting its distinctive buildings will be a challenge for the future.

The view that Dickinson captures in his drawing, showing both the Capitol's dome and the Washington Monument, in addition to the tiered tower of the AFHR's Forwood building on the far left, has changed over time. Now only the tip of the Forwood's tower peeks through thick trees, and more trees obscure the monument. The Capitol still pokes up on the horizon, hazily, and its actual position relative to the monument suggests that Dickinson used creative license in his rendering. The Forwood building was constructed in 1903–1906, to serve as a hospital. Its elaborate tower replicates Philadelphia's Independence Hall and also houses one of the oldest veteran's surgical theater suits in the country. Today the building is outdated and in need of restoration for another use, if it is to be saved.

Soldiers' Home.

Aerial view of the Armed
Forces Retirement Home
(Soldier's Home), early 1990s.
Photo courtesy of the Armed
Forces Retirement Home,
Public Affairs Office.

Maryland and Virginia Sites

Northwest Branch: Northwest Mills to Burnt Mills. **Robert Shosteck, Guide to Trails around Washington. © Robert Shosteck, 1937.**

Adelphi (Riggs) Mill

Dickinson probably discovered the Northwest Branch trail that leads from Burnt Mills to the still-standing Adelphi Mill, also known as Riggs Mill, after the prominent Washington Riggs family who owned the mill from 1865 to 1920, for he sketched both mills. The Rambler may even have accompanied him on this sketching trek, for the area was well known to the *Evening Star* journalist who wrote in one of his columns: "From the mill there is a well worn trail which leads to the ancient rocks above the mill and the rushing and roaring waters of the branch. High up there, with great broad rock masses and just enough soil to support a growth of trees, many people from the city go to enjoy the scene and eat their lunches."[1]

This beautiful stone mill may be the oldest and largest mill in the Washington area. Built around 1796 by Issachar and Mahlon Scholfield, the mill continued grinding corn and wheat well into the twentieth century. Today the restored mill belongs to the Maryland-National Capital Park and Planning Commission and can be rented for weddings or other events. The exterior water wheel seen in Dickinson's drawing has been removed. During the nineteenth century, Thomas Sheckels, and later his grandson William H. Freeman, ran the mill, and it was sometimes referred to as Freeman's Mill. When Dickinson made his drawing, George Washington Riggs, founder of Riggs and Company, owned the mill, though the Freeman family continued to operate it until 1911. The last miller's daughter, Helen Powell, shared memories with a local journalist in 1999, when she was ninety-three years old:

> I was born there in the miller's house…. My father [Lynn Freeman] run the mill…. On Monday, the [farmers] would come down [to the mill] with wagon loads of grains, corn and wheat. Then they'd come back at the end of the week and pick up the ground flour, mashed up for meal for horses and cows and chickens…. It was farm all the way to the District. Oh, there was just nothing around here. Riggs Road was stone, gravel.[2]

The mill stands on the Northwest branch about five miles above where that branch flows into the Eastern branch [today's Anacostia River] near Bladensburg road, and Mr. Freeman [the blacksmith] remembers having often heard …that ships used to come up as far as the mill and that they often brought brick in ballust, taking back a return cargo of flour. —The Rambler, *Evening Star*, June 7, 1914

Riggs Mill.

Dear Ted,

Mother and I had a most lovely ride the other day, way up beyond Sligo Creek to what is called Northwest Branch, at Burnt Mills, where is a beautiful gorge, deep and narrow, with great boulders and even cliffs. Excepting Great Falls it is the most beautiful place around here.
—President Theodore Roosevelt to his son, June 21, 1904

Burnt Mills, Maryland.

Burnt Mills

Many people wonder if the name Burnt Mills comes from an old mill that burned down on the site. In fact, old-timers from the Burnt Mills community have passed down this very story, but the name appears frequently as a general mill name on both sides of the Potomac, so that its origins remain obscure.

Burnt Mills, no longer extant, stood on both sides of Colesville Road (once called the turnpike and Columbia Pike). The dam across the Northwest Branch was on the west side of the road and the mill on the east. The dam is still there and is a prominent feature of Burnt Mills Park, maintained by the Maryland-National Capital Park and Planning Commission. The mill property, originally called Mill Seat, was owned by Samuel Beall Jr. from 1745 to the early 1800s, after which it passed to a chain of owners, and finally ceased operation around 1921. It was torn down in 1928. An unfinished manuscript by John Rodgers Beall in 1931 describes the mill's beneficial location:

> The gorge in which the mill lies provides one of the best locations for a water power mill in the section. The stream has a sufficiently rapid fall to provide the necessary head of water without an overly long race. A wide curve in the stream at this point allows further shortening of the race. Lastly, the formation of the land is such that a comparatively small dam will impound a large quantity of water.[3]

Visitors today can admire the stream's large, tumbled boulders in the winding streambed. The Rambler wrote that "the Northwest branch has scoured down through soil of the weathered rocks deep into the basin rock.... It is because of this deep cutting that the Northwest branch presents such allurements for a hard walk."[4] These allurements remain and so do the trails, which Robert Shosteck's Northwest Branch map from the 1930s shows (page 127).

The boulders and dam at Burnt Mills, all that's left of the mill site today. Photos © 2011 Joseph Spilsbury.

Mount Vernon

In 1918, Robert L. Dickinson made his way to the spacious lawns and Potomac lookout of Mount Vernon, home of President George Washington.[5] For more than one hundred years before Dickinson's visit, and even during Washington's own lifetime, Americans and foreigners had been making pilgrimages to the Father of the Country's homestead. Though many of these visitors and dignitaries brought gifts, few left behind such a charming record as Dickinson's drawings. Of his three Mount Vernon sketches, two focus on the upper garden, one showing the small "schoolhouse" where Washington's stepchildren, Nelly and Washy, are said to have had lessons. The other pavilion across the garden was a "necessary," or outhouse.

In Dickinson's day Mount Vernon, south of Alexandria, could be reached by rail, steamboat, or "sight-seeing cars." Beginning in the 1930s, the graceful George Washington Memorial Parkway was built, linking the historic home to Great Falls, Virginia, site of Washington's Patowmack Canal Company (see chapter one).

The estate and gardens Dickinson visited in 1918 had been evolving since 1858, when the Mount Vernon Ladies' Association, led by Ann Pamela Cunningham, purchased the rundown property from John Augustine Washington—the property's third heir following Martha Washington's death in 1802—and undertook its restoration. Work on the upper and lower gardens flanking the bowling green in front of the mansion did not begin until the early 1950s; thus, the garden sketched by Dickinson in 1918 had been modified over the century following the president's death in 1799. The Ladies' Association's mission has been to restore the home and estate to its 1799 peak under Washington's ownership. In Dickinson's rendering of the upper flower garden, the original wall footings had endured, helping maintain the garden's cozy feel over decades of change. The current flowers reflect varieties common to Virginia gardens during Washington's era. Boxwood plants surviving from 1798 were critical to identifying the original paths and beds during the restoration. According to estate historians:

> In the 18th century box was used both as a border and as a hedge. Around the individual flower beds the box was certainly kept trimmed down to six inches or so; otherwise their formal designs—fleur-de-lis, lozenges, spirals and the like—would not have been perceptible. Most of the box at Mount Vernon was planted in 1798, and as it is slow growing it could not have reached its present height in Washington's lifetime.

No estate in the United America is more pleasantly situated than this. It lies in a high, dry, and healthy country...one of the finest rivers in the world.
—George Washington, 1793

Portraits of George and Martha Washington by Gilbert Stuart
(1755–1828). Oil on canvas, 1796. 129.9 x 94cm (48 x 37 in.) each.
National Portrait Gallery, Smithsonian Institution; owned jointly
with the Museum of Fine Arts, Boston, NPG.80.115, NPG.80.116.

The buds of every kind of tree and shrub are swelling—the tender leaves of many had unfolded—the apricot blossoms were putting forth—the peaches and cherries were upon the point of doing the same. The leaves of the apple trees were coming out, those of the weeping willows and the lilac had been out many days and were the first to show themselves.... The red bud had begun to open...the dogwood had swelled into buttons.—George Washington, April 16, 1785

It is possible that the present "closed effect" is correct, and that something else was used for screening. It is known that in eighteenth-century formal gardens privacy was sought. Living conditions inside the plantation houses made it desirable, for with the constant presence of visitors and the great numbers of servants needed when everything was made by hand, indoor privacy was a rarity.[6]

Washington was an avid horticulturist and personally designed and supervised the planting of his gardens. He divided his 2,700-acre estate (that grew to 8,000 acres by the time of his death) into five working farms with overseers and slaves for each. The Mansion House Farm of 500 acres was the one surrounding his home and today more or less comprises the historic site, with only 30 acres open to the public. Washington's favorite way to spend his time was managing his plantation, and he made daily rounds of the farms. When away from home for years as commander of the Continental Army and as president, he corresponded with his manager on a weekly basis. He liked being called the First Farmer in America and Farmer Washington, and his estate was considered an agricultural laboratory that employed Britain's latest "theories of soil and cultivation and stock breeding.... Plants, seeds, and cuttings were imported from Europe, while many more were received from friends, both at home and abroad."[7] Washington freely admitted that his love for gentleman farming exceeded his happiness as a leader. Although the estate was never profitable except in its land value, its development and management refreshed Washington following the demanding responsibilities of public life. His "bountiful hospitality" meant enlarging the house and raising provisions for entertaining on a grand scale. Yet, none of this stimulating, aristocratic lifestyle would have been possible without hundreds of slaves. Even with slaves, the president found Mount Vernon's constant entertaining a financial burden, and within fifty years of his death, the continued lifestyle virtually bankrupted his heirs, who "were like people living in a museum, which they had to maintain at their own expense."[8] Visitors streamed to visit the popular president's home and tomb, just as they had streamed to visit the president during his lifetime. "[T]he hospitality imposed upon the owners was a heavy drain on resources...they found it impossible to make even the most necessary repairs."[9] More than two hundred years after Washington's death, the colonial mansion and grounds are meticulously maintained for those paying homage to the country's first, revered leader and plantation owner. Through this remarkable preservation, a cruel chapter in American history—slavery—is clearly exhibited to the visitor, another educational purpose of the site.

A profile of Mount Vernon, 1918.

MOUNT VERNON
THE GARDEN 1918

Mount Vernon,
the garden, 1918.

The "School House,"
Mount Vernon garden, 1918.

Mount Vernon began as a 5,000-acre estate granted by Lord Culpeper in 1674 to Nicholas Spencer and John Washington, great-grandfather of George. Its first name was Little Hunting Creek Plantation. In 1690, the land was divided between the Spencer and Washington heirs, with the 2,500-acre Mount Vernon tract going to John's son Lawrence, who left it to his daughter Mildred. She sold it in 1726 to her brother Augustine, and he built the original house in 1734. Augustine's son Lawrence, George's older half-brother, inherited the property when their father died in 1743. He and his bride Anne Fairfax renamed the estate Mount Vernon, in honor of the English admiral Edward Vernon, under whom Lawrence had served against the Spanish in the Caribbean "War of Jenkins Ear." Around 1747, teenage George took up residence with his brother and sister-in-law. When Lawrence died in 1752, with his infant heir Sarah dying a few months later, George began renting the property from his sister-in-law. Upon her death in 1761, he inherited the estate. As a soldier stationed far away during the French and Indian War, George did not tend to his Mount Vernon property until his marriage to Martha Dandridge Custis in 1759, when both were in their late twenties. Martha, a widow with two young children, came to the marriage with considerable wealth and slaveholdings that proved essential to Mount Vernon's large-scale development. George and Martha had no children of their own—George may well have been infertile as a result of a tuberculosis infection contracted as a young man.[10] Martha's children, raised at Mount Vernon, died young—Patsy of epilepsy at age seventeen and Jacky (John Parke Custis) of "camp fever," sadly while serving as an aide to General Washington during the siege of Yorktown in 1781. Two of Jack's four young children came to live at Mount Vernon and were raised there: Nelly and George Washington Parke Custis, the latter of whom built the Arlington estate (now Arlington Cemetery). His only daughter, Mary Anna Randolph Custis, married Robert E. Lee (see page 140).

The heirs inheriting Mount Vernon from the Washington line were Bushrod, a nephew and associate justice of the Supreme Court; John Augustine, Bushrod's nephew; and finally, his son, John Augustine Jr., who sold the estate in 1858 to the Mount Vernon Ladies' Association, under whose supervision the immaculately restored estate remains.

WITH THE RAMBLER

Citizen of Fairfax County

Very many persons seem to think that George Washington is merely a marble statue or perhaps an effigy in bronze. To others he is a national saint, who always appears in public dressed in a ghostly toga, or...a raised sword in one hand, a scroll of parchment in the other and a halo around his head.

They do not seem to grasp the fact that George Washington was a human being, and a very human being; that he raised sheep, wheat and corn in Fairfax county; that he lived in that county from boyhood until his death, except for absence due to the call of his country; that he swapped jokes and gossip with his county neighbors at church and at sundry taverns; that he visited his friends and was visited by them....

One should not get an impression from the foregoing lines that George Washington's neighbors in Fairfax county did not know the bigness of his character or the nobility of his nature, and that they did not early acknowledge his eminence and then his pre-eminence among them. They did, but it seems to be a fact that many Americans find it hard to get away from the thought that George Washington was a superman, usually astride a brass horse or forever making speeches to the house of burgesses, the congress of the Continental army about taxation, representation, independence and patriotism.

They cannot think of George Washington as a citizen of Fairfax county who might climb a rail fence, walk across a field to where an old black [man] was plowing and say in a perfectly natural and unoratorical voice, "Uncle Nace, you ain't runnin' that furrow straight." —The Rambler, *Evening Star,* May 19, 1918

Tomb of the Unknown Soldier, Arlington Cemetery

As Dickinson explored Washington, he paid a visit to Arlington Cemetery's tranquil hilltop and sketched the Unknown Soldier's tomb. The grave must have held particular meaning for Dickinson, for it symbolized his own reason for being in Washington—World War I and its terrible death toll.

Dickinson sketched the tomb at an interesting moment in its development. Both the grave and the elaborate Memorial Amphitheatre behind it had been under construction for several years but were not dedicated with an actual "unknown's" remains until November 1921, several years after Dickinson's departure. The elaborate, white marble sarcophagus weighing fifty tons was placed over the grave in 1926, making it difficult to recognize today's tomb in Dickinson's drawing. Although an anonymous soldier was selected and interred there, he represents "all the unknowns who died in brave service to our country during World War I."[11]

During his pilgrimage to the grave, Dickinson likely visited the cemetery's golden-columned Arlington House, General Robert E. Lee's home before the Civil War. On its green hilltop that commands a spectacular view of the Potomac and capital city, Arlington House might be Washington's loveliest setting. Today, the house faces the Lincoln Memorial, which was still under construction when Dickinson drew the tomb. In architect Charles McKim's original 1901 design for the Lincoln Memorial, both the front and back of the building were open, as the front is today; Henry Bacon's 1911 redesign sealed off the back that faces Arlington House.

In 1925, Arlington House was designated a permanent memorial to Robert E. Lee, and it reopened to the public in 1929. In 1933, the National Park Service took over its jurisdiction from the War Department.

Dickinson probably knew the sad story about the last owners of Arlington House—Robert E. Lee and his wife, Mary Anna Randolph Custis, who had inherited the house from her father, George Washington Parke Custis, grandson of the first president and his wife (see Mount Vernon, page 132).

George Washington Parke Custis emulated his grandfather George Washington and over his lifetime sought to create a museum and memorial to the first president. He built Arlington House and filled it with Washington memorabilia. He wanted to name the mansion Mount Washington, but relatives convinced him to name it after the family's original Arlington estate on Virginia's eastern shore.

Custis's only surviving daughter, Mary Anna, married Robert E. Lee in 1831. For the next thirty years, Arlington House served as the Lees' home base, as Lee was a military officer posted outside of Washington. Some of his assignments included supervising an engineering project in St. Louis, Missouri's

The Unknown Soldier's grave.

harbor; serving in the Mexican War under General Winfield Scott; superintending West Point's military academy; commanding the Second U.S. Cavalry in Texas; and leading a detachment that captured John Brown in Harper's Ferry in 1859. Although Lee managed Arlington House after his father-in-law's death, he never owned it.[12]

Many generations have passed since the Civil War hostilities, and most visitors to today's national burial ground on the peaceful hill above the Potomac marvel at its beauty and tribute to those who died for their country. They are not necessarily aware of the tragic Civil War events that led to Arlington's becoming a military cemetery. The grave sites of leaders or achievers naturally attract visitors— President John F. Kennedy and Senator Robert Kennedy, President William Howard Taft, Secretary of State William Jennings Bryan, Supreme Court Justice William O. Douglas, Secretary of State John Foster Dulles, novelist Dashiell Hammett, Supreme Court Justice Oliver Wendell Holmes Jr., Peter Charles L'Enfant, Robert Todd Lincoln, and composer Ignace Jan Paderewski, to name just a few. The 612 gracefully landscaped acres also house numerous memorials and monuments dedicated to historic events, including the Spanish-American War, the Rough Riders, Pearl Harbor, the Vietnam War, and various tombs to Unknown Soldiers. Women are also honored at the cemetery.

The story of Arlington transforming from a private residence to a national cemetery is one of war and human loss. Historians have recorded how at the start of the Civil War, Lee was deeply pained at having to choose between his country and his state. He had devoted more than thirty years to his country as a loyal army officer, and his family's heritage was entwined with the founding of the United States. On the day he resigned from the military, shortly after Virginia's vote to secede from the Union, Lee wrote his sister, "With all my devotion to the Union and the feeling of loyalty and duty as an American citizen, I have not been able to make up my mind to raise my hand against my relatives, my children, my home."[13] After his decision to remain loyal to Virginia, Lee was called to Richmond and appointed commander of the state's forces, although Virginia had not yet joined the Confederacy. Lee wrote his wife to flee to safer territory, knowing the strategic position of Arlington House for the federal army. Mary Custis Lee moved heirloom paintings and silver but left everything else in the house, not expecting her personal property to be touched. Within days, federal troops made the house a Union army headquarters. Heirlooms of the Washington, Custis, and Lee families quickly disappeared before Brigadier General Irvin McDowell issued an order for Lee's remaining possessions to be stored at the Patent Office. In addition to the headquarters at Arlington House, Fort Whipple (today's Fort Myer) and Fort McPherson were established on the Lees' property. Lee wrote to his wife: "It is better to make up our minds to a general loss. They cannot take away the remembrance of the spot, and the memories of those that to us rendered it sacred. That will remain to us as long as life will last, and that we can preserve."[14]

In order to confiscate Confederate private property, Congress passed a tax law in June 1862 that required legal title holders to appear in person to pay an insurrectionary property tax based on a government commission's assessment of the property's value. Similar to other Confederate landowners, Mary Custis Lee was unable to pay the tax without risking arrest. Also, her semi-invalid condition would have made the trip difficult. Her cousin went to Alexandria to pay the tax for her but was refused. Thus, as stipulated by the new tax law, Arlington went up for sale at a public auction attended only by the tax commissioners.[15] Once under government ownership, the house fell under the jurisdiction of Secretary of War Edwin M. Stanton, because it was a military post. Quartermaster General of the army Montgomery Meigs, of earlier Cabin John Bridge fame (see page 81), had direct control of the property, and his dealings with the Lee house showed how war can affect human actions. His handling of the cemetery was probably influenced by the loss of his son, a Union soldier killed by "Southern guerillas," as he reportedly said. Stanton shared Meigs's "deep hatred for the Southerners who left the Union" and supported Meigs's policies.[16]

By 1864, national burial ground was desperately needed in Washington, and Stanton ordered Meigs to survey possible sites. Meigs apparently made no surveys at all, but sent word to Stanton that Arlington's grounds were ideally suited to the purpose. Stanton approved Meigs's plan. Within the estate's more than 1,000 acres, the quartermaster general chose the acreage surrounding the Lee mansion for the new cemetery; a month earlier he had already buried more than a dozen soldiers nearby, perhaps to create a precedent. When Meigs later inspected the new burials he had ordered, he found the graves too far from the house and had them moved closer to "Mrs. Lee's once famous rose garden only yards from the house. Those graves remain in their original locations and can be seen today encircling the restored garden."[17] Meigs's actions did not stop with the rose garden intrusion. A few years later he commissioned a large stone vault for the unknown dead to be built in the garden, where it still stands. Finally, Meigs himself is buried close to the rose garden, along with his wife, father, and son.[18]

Some time after the Lees' death, their son George Lee filed a claim against the United States for the recovery of the family property or for just compensation. Five years later, in 1882, the case reached the U.S. Supreme Court, which decided in Lee's favor, citing that "the United States had denied Mary Custis Lee her property without due process when its tax commissioners had refused to accept the payment of taxes from anyone but the owner." Congress then appropriated $150,000 to compensate Lee, and "Arlington became the official National Cemetery of the United States of America."[19]

In 1901, the Senate Park Commission Report, known as the blueprint for Washington's beautification, included a few paragraphs on Arlington Cemetery's future development, urging a landscape based on "simplicity and uniformity" unmarred by "the monstrosities which dominate in all modern cemeteries." The report warned that pretentious tombstones, even though erected out of love, "disturb those very ideas of peace and quiet which should characterize a spot sacred to the tenderest feelings of the human heart." The document even made a passionate plea for preservation of the cemetery's "noble slopes toward the river [that] should be vigorously protected against the invasion of monuments which utterly annihilate the sense of beauty and repose. This is one of the most beautiful spots in the vicinity of Washington; it should not be defaced or touched in any way, and a law or rule should at once be passed forbidding the placing of any monument on this hill."[20] As often happens, the advice was not heeded, and soon the Memorial Amphitheatre and ostentatious Memorial Gate appeared on the noble slopes. But perhaps such additions are inevitable at the foremost shrine to our nation's heroes.

Fairfax County Courthouse

The Fairfax Courthouse moved three times but has remained in its present Fairfax City location for more than two hundred years. Although now surrounded by Northern Virginia's sprawl, with newer municipal buildings crowding in, the courthouse's historic attributes have been preserved.

Fairfax County, named for Thomas, the sixth Lord Fairfax, was formed in 1742, with its courthouse located at "Spring Fields," near the county's present-day commercial core at Tyson's Corner. In Colonial Virginia, county courthouses served several political and economic roles besides administering justice, and within their walls the business of managing local affairs was generally conducted. Court days were well attended. "Business at court brought many to the county seat; many others came because it was a time to see friends and transact private business."[21]

Scholars have pointed out that the colonial New England village green and the Virginia courthouse square share historical roots: both were British colonial settlements whose architectural, political, and cultural traditions influenced how later towns developed. "[T]he village green was the setting for town meeting hall and church while the Virginia square began typically as a civic center and market place serving a rural population."[22]

Rising merchants succeeded in obtaining relocation of the county seat to Alexandria in 1752, attracted by the town's prospect of becoming a thriving seaport and commercial center. Court business at Spring Fields concluded in May 1752, and a new courthouse in Alexandria opened in December 1754.

Fairfax Court House, where G[eorge]
W[ashington]'s will is kept.

In the interim, the court conducted business in temporary quarters nearby, and its records note the names of George Washington, George Mason, and other colonial notables as conducting business there, which included elections to the Virginia House of Burgesses.

After the Revolutionary War, with the courthouse in need of serious repair and with plans for the new national capital to encompass Alexandria, Fairfax County decided to relocate its county seat to a central location, a town called Providence, but more often known as Fairfax Court House. James Wren designed the building in "a style reminiscent of the colonial capital at Williamsburg and of eighteenth-century English towns and market halls." The handsome brick building was occupied in 1800. "Its gabled roof was topped by a cupola for a bell to announce the convening of the court. The two-story height of the building gave the courtroom the proportions of a church nave."[23]

The Civil War took its toll on the building, which both the Confederate and Union troops occupied at various times. It was used mainly as an aid station and lookout post. The interior was gutted and valuable records were stolen or destroyed. County government changes after the war moved legal proceedings away from the courts to supervisory boards, and circuit courts took over judicial proceedings. During the courthouse's postwar rehabilitation, a new two-story office building replaced an earlier clerk's office that had burned down, and the new design "with the popular Victorian preference for dentils, cornices, corbelling, and pilasters" was intended to work well with Wren's original functional design.[24] The first addition to the courthouse came after Dickinson's time, in 1929, when an annex was added to the back of the building; a second addition came in 1954, and both additions harmonized with the original architectural style. In 1969, as a result of significant population growth, the county built a twelve-story office building next to the courthouse lot, taking care not to "encroach upon or dominate the old courthouse and former jail, which stand, as they have throughout the years, overlooking a major crossroads, shaded by ancient trees with their stone-enclosed green." Virginia historian Ross D. Netherton has written that today's courthouse "maintains a nineteenth-century interior design and furnishings, and continues in daily use as one of the county's regular courts for certain categories of cases and for ceremonial events."[25]

Civil War Forts

When Dickinson visited Forts Ward and Barnard in 1918, they were already sixty-year-old ruins. Today, Washington's Civil War forts are almost 150 years old, but many can still be found hidden in the landscape. The original earthwork forts, whose trenches Dickinson captures in his Fort Barnard drawing, are now grass-covered mounds that blend in with the natural surroundings, and in the case of Fort Barnard, nothing remains at all. The fort became a public park and playground at the intersection of today's South Pollard Street and Walter Reed Drive in Arlington. Fort Ward became a City of Alexandria historic site, and as a result, underwent extensive reconstruction that includes a museum with interpretive programs. Arlington's Fort Whipple was the only defense site to become a permanent military establishment—today's Fort Myer.

On April 12, 1861, the Civil War began with the battle of Fort Sumter. To preserve the Union, President Lincoln immediately called for 75,000 volunteer soldiers. This action spurred Virginia to secede from the Union, causing the Lincoln administration to seize strategic military footholds in Alexandria and Arlington Heights, Virginia. Union manpower went rapidly into constructing earthen defense posts to protect Washington, but the city remained vulnerable. Over the ensuing four-year war, additional forts, batteries, and rifle trenches were built, until Washington had one of the largest fort systems in the world.

The Union army's defeat at the Battle of Bull Run (Manassas) in July 1861 demonstrated the urgent need for a well-trained army and far greater fortification for Washington. Major (later Brevet Major General) John Gross Barnard of the Army Corps of Engineers assumed leadership of the city's defense system. A commission formed to study the enemy's possible approaches to the city and soon reported that a defense system for Washington could be divided into four groups of fortifications: those south of the Potomac from Fort Lyon below Alexandria to Fort DeKalb (Fort Strong) opposite Georgetown; those related to Chain Bridge; those north of the Potomac from Fort Sumner to Fort Lincoln; and those south of the Eastern Branch (Anacostia River) from Fort Mahan to Fort Greble.[26]

Barnard's report described Fort Barnard as occupying a commanding position. "It covers the head of ravines, in which large bodies of troops can be collected and concealed in a favorable position for making flank attacks upon an enemy's columns assaulting our lines between it and Fort Craig, or attempting to penetrate the valley of Four-Mile Run. Taken in connection with its outworks and rifle-trenches, the ground

Fort Barnard trenches. At top:
The hills are beyond the Potomac
River—Alexandria trolley.

may be considered well occupied, though the work itself is rather small." Fort Ward occupied an even more important position for it defended the Leesburg and Alexandria Turnpike (today's Route 7), in addition to connecting roads, and also overlooked "the country northwardly and westwardly towards Fort DeKalb and towards Bailey's and Ball's Cross Roads."[27]

When forts went up, trees came down and played an important role in defending an outpost, for the outward facing branches made passage impossible. One eyewitness of the tree-felling process wrote:

> [T]he choppers would begin at the foot of the hill, the line extending for perhaps a mile, and cut only part way through the tree, and in this way work up to the crest, leaving the top row so that a single blow would bring down the tree—then, when all was ready, the bugle would sound as a signal, and the last stroke of the axe be given, which brought down the top row; these falling on those below would bring them down, and…the forest would fall with a crash like mighty thunder.[28]

By the end of the war in 1865, 68 forts, 93 batteries, and 837 guns in rifle trenches protected Washington in a connected defense system. Thirty miles of military roads joined these fortifications.

The intense effort to build and refine Washington's circle of defenses resulted in unpleasant and often dangerous conditions for the homeowners living under Union occupation. Anne S. Frobel's Civil War diary gives an almost daily account of her struggles dealing with Union soldiers on her farm south of Alexandria.[29]

Army of the Potomac veterans looking back on their duty in the defenses of Washington sometimes described it as a "soft assignment."[30] In the end, Washington passed a surprisingly safe Civil War. Only one battle occurred, when Confederate Lieutenant General Jubal A. Early led an attack from the north on Fort Stevens in July of 1864. The timing was considered right, for Lieutenant General Ulysses S. Grant's progress in the South at Petersburg, Virginia, had required reinforcement from Washington's well-trained artillery regiments, who were then replaced by new recruits. Only about 9,000 soldiers defended the city's entire defense ring in early July. Southern leaders hoped their attack would cause panic and relieve pressure on General Lee's lines at Petersburg. Early's forces of 14,000 men crossed the Potomac River and ransomed Frederick, Maryland, for $200,000. Early's troops then defeated a Union force commanded by Major General Lew Wallace near the Monacacy River close to Frederick. Grant immediately sent reinforcements for

Washington. Unbearable heat delayed Early's march to Washington's northern Forts Stevens, Slocum, and DeRussy, which allowed time for the Union reinforcements to arrive in July of 1864. Lieutenant General Early saw his predicament—he was isolated from Lee's army, with diminishing routes of retreat as more Union soldiers arrived. On July 12, at Fort Stevens, he engaged in fire, but as soon as it was dark, retreated to Virginia.

At the end of the war in 1865, the forts were dismantled for their valuable materials, including wood, and most of the land was returned to prewar owners. Many freed slaves lived in squatters' villages near the forts, and they never received adequate help with resettlement and housing. Many of Tenleytown's African Americans at Fort Reno were able to afford the five-dollar down payment when the land on which their rustic dwellings stood went up for sale. Over the decades, their settlement prospered and became integrated with whites, though the blacks attended separate schools and churches. In the 1920s and 30s, this stable community with strong black representation was displaced by white suburban development. Most of the black residents moved to the segregated side of Washington, east of Rock Creek Park.[31]

Today, the National Park Service and the National Capital Parks East oversee a number of the former forts. Those with partial reconstruction include Fort Stevens, Fort Ward, and Ford Foote. Fort Ward—named for Commander James Harmon Ward, from Hartford, Connecticut, the first Union naval officer killed in the war—offers bus tours to several of the fascinating forts encircling Washington.[32]

The Civil War Defenses of Washington. Courtesy the National Park Service, National Capital Region.

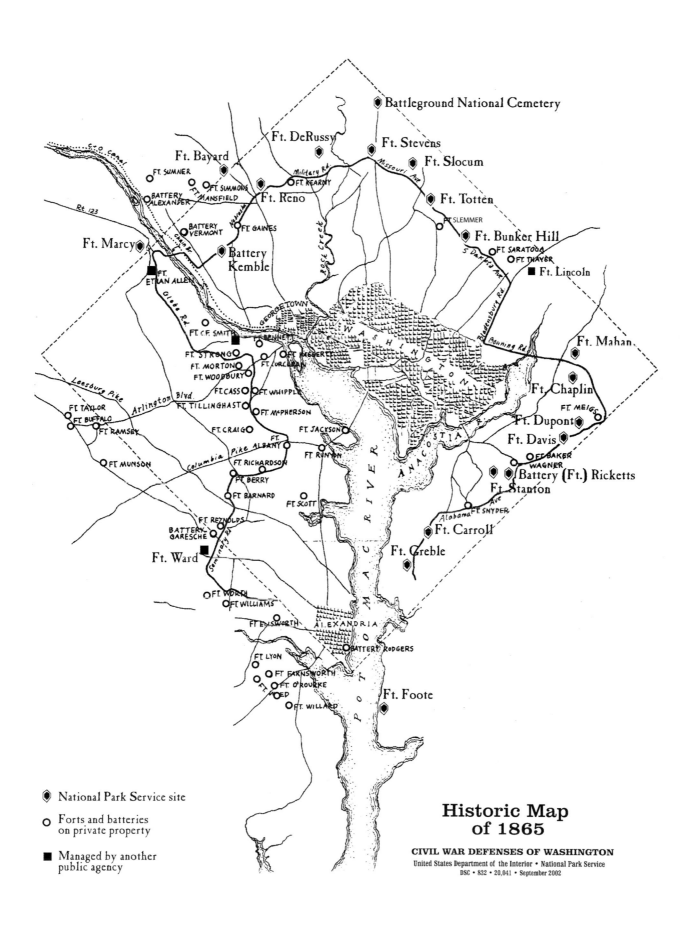

Battleground National Cemetery

Ft. DeRussy

Ft. Bayard

Ft. Stevens

Ft. Slocum

FT. SUMNER

Military Rd.

Mssouri Ave.

FT. SUMMONS

FT. KEARNY

FT. MANSFIELD

BATTERY ALEXANDER

Rt. 123

Ft. Reno

Ft. Totten

FT. SLEMMER

BATTERY VERMONT

FT. GAINES

Ft. Bunker Hill

FT. SARATOGA

Ft. Marcy

FT. THAYER

Battery Kemble

FT. ETHAN ALLEN

Ft. Lincoln

Glebe Rd.

GEORGETOWN

WASHINGTON

Ft. Mahan

FT. C.F. SMITH

Ft. Chaplin

FT. STRONG

FT. MIGBERT

FT. MORTON

FT. CORCORAN

FT. WOODBURY

FT. MEIGS

FT. CASS

FT. WHIPPLE

Leesburg Pike

Arlington Blvd.

Ft. Dupont

FT. TAYLOR

FT. TILLINGHAST

FT. McPHERSON

Ft. Davis

FT. BUFFALO

FT. BAKER

FT. RAMSEY

FT. CRAIG

FT. JACKSON

WAGNER

Pike

FT. ALBANY

Battery (Ft.) Ricketts

FT. MUNSON

Columbia

FT. RICHARDSON

FT. RUNYON

Ft. Stanton

FT. BERRY

E. SNYDER

Ave.

FT. BARNARD

FT. SCOTT

Alabama

Ft. Carroll

FT. REYNOLDS

BATTERY GARESCHE

Ft. Greble

Ft. Ward

FT. WORTH

FT. WILLIAMS

FT. ELLSWORTH

ALEXANDRIA

BATTERY RODGERS

FT. LYON

FT. FARNSWORTH

FT. O'ROURKE

FT. WEED

Ft. Foote

FT. WILLARD

◈ National Park Service site

○ Forts and batteries on private property

■ Managed by another public agency

Historic Map of 1865

CIVIL WAR DEFENSES OF WASHINGTON

United States Department of the Interior • National Park Service
DSC • 832 • 20,041 • September 2002

Washington from Fort Ward. At top:
Navy radio—Monument and Post—
Union Station—Capitol—Congressional
Library; second line: Fort Barnard—
Fort Reynolds (dark trees) Fort Scott.

Robert Latou Dickinson

ROBERT LATOU DICKINSON

obert Latou Dickinson's (1861–1950) long life and medical career encompassed many phases and achievements, including an eighteen-month military tour of duty in Washington, DC, during World War I. An accomplished artist from childhood, Dickinson left behind a sketchbook of delightful Washington, DC, landscapes that he intended to include in a trail book called "A Washington Walk Book," which would be similar to the *New York Walk Book* he coauthored and illustrated for the American Geographic Society during the same period.

Dickinson was a man of unusual talent. As a precocious fourteen-year-old pursuing a European education, he wrote letters home filled with sophisticated observations about the art, culture, and traditions surrounding him. As a young obstetrician and gynecologist in New York City in the late 1800s, he rapidly gained a reputation as a surgeon, teacher, writer, and hospital organizer. His caring clinical work with women patients led to advocacy of birth control, reform of Victorian sexual mores, research in the nascent field of marriage counseling, and new teaching models for medical students. He wrote and illustrated medical textbooks in his field and was co-sculptor of educational models that depicted conception and birth.

In the second phase of his long career, from the 1920s until his death, Dickinson was the medical profession's leader of the contraceptive movement and eventually allied himself with Margaret Sanger's cause, which culminated in the Planned Parenthood organization. As if seventy years of prodigious, groundbreaking activity in the public health and medical fields were not a sufficient lifetime contribution, Dickinson accomplished more. Tapping into his abundant creativity and spiritual depth, he translated his deep appreciation for the natural world into landscape drawings to bring the joys of nature to his family, friends, and the public. His illustrations of rivers and mountains for the *New York Walk Book* of 1923 have appeared in subsequent editions to the present day. The original book starts out with a Dickinsonian message:

> Fortunate we are that in civilization lurks the antidote to civilization—that strain in the blood of all of us, of cave man and tree man, nomad and seaman, chopper and digger, fisher and trailer, crying out to this call of the earth, to this tug of free foot, up-and-over, to this clamor for out-and-beyond. Happy are we, in our day, harking back to this call, to be part of an ozone revival that fits the growth of our desire, to see the beginning of a break-away into everybody's out-of-doors, and the happy find of a wide, fair wilderness.[1]

Self-portrait, Robert Latou Dickinson, at age seventy. Courtesy Ian Barbour.

A WASHINGTON WALK BOOK

by Robert Latou Dickinson

The American Geographical
Society ~ Broadway at
156th Street New York
1922.

Dickinson also wrote and illustrated a Palisades Interstate Park booklet, produced maps, sketched the Adirondacks and the White Mountains, perfected an original lettering style, designed monograms and bookplates, and documented the array of Chinese boats he witnessed during a Public Health Service mission to China in 1919.

The short introduction to Dickinson's life that follows covers his pioneering contributions in his chosen fields of gynecology and birth control advocacy. A section on his war years in Washington, DC, begins on page 166.

Early Life

Robert L. Dickinson was born on February 21, 1861, in Jersey City, New Jersey, where his mother, Jennette Latou (d. 1924), of Mamaroneck, New York, had gone for the day to lunch with her sister. Both sides of the family—the Dickinsons and Latous—had prospered in the United States. Dickinson's father, Horace Dickinson II (1824–1901), was partner in a Mamaroneck hat factory with his brother-in-law William E. Doubleday, father of publishing magnate Frank Doubleday, who was Robert Dickinson's age and playmate growing up. Robert Dickinson was the oldest of Horace and Jennette's three surviving children.

At age ten, Dickinson had a canoe accident in the Adirondacks that made him decide to become a doctor. He and his father had built a canoe and took it out for a test run. While his father paddled the boat, Dickinson stood in the water facing it, to judge its performance. An unexpected current swung the canoe into him. He later described the accident to his family:

> The stem was of galvanized iron, with the top bent over sharply so that the point was as sharp as a knife. That's what I hit…I got an eight inch tear across my tummy, but held my bowels in and swam ashore….They took me to a house and carried me indoors. The doctor was so crippled with arthritis he couldn't do anything. So the carpenter had to do it and put in the stitches but missed some things, so I am a little lopsided…. I was eight weeks in bed and when I got up I collapsed on the floor. But that man I adored so, that doctor—that's what I wanted to be, a doctor.[2]

In the early 1870s, the Dickinson-Doubleday hat factory burned down, and for relief from the crisis, the Dickinson family took a one-year trip to Europe but ended up staying four years. After the first summer touring France and England, the three Dickinson children attended school in Geneva while their parents continued traveling. The family reunited for holidays. Later the boys attended school in Germany. While living abroad, Dickinson began writing and illustrating his first diary, a habit that continued for the rest of his life, although a Washington, DC, diary is not among his collected papers.

Dickinson's sketch for the title page of his future Washington Walk Book.

When the family returned to the States, Dickinson enrolled in the Brooklyn Polytechnic Institute for a premed, liberal arts curriculum. The family lived at 165 State Street in an adjoining house to the Doubleday relatives. One late winter night, Frank and Rob, about age seventeen, climbed the Brooklyn Bridge's east tower, while the bridge was still under construction, ascending one of the main cables, using a separate hand cable to steady themselves. According to family history, "Close to the tower, the going became steeper, and to get to the very top they had to surmount a projecting cornice. The real test was the descent, which began with a drop over the cornice edge onto the cable which they could not see below them."[3]

Outdoor adventures began at an early age for Dickinson. His early canoe injury had affected his throwing ability, but otherwise he was agile and athletic throughout his life. His family recalls that at age eighty-five he could still do a back flip from the high dive and also dive into a lake across two canoes moored at the dock. When he began to practice as a doctor in Brooklyn, he rode a bicycle, not only for transportation but also for long outdoor excursions. Throughout life he was an avid sailor, hiker, and canoer, and his enthusiasm for such activities was contagious.

From 1879 to 1881, Dickinson attended the Long Island College Hospital (LICH). It was a new medical school and prided itself on following the European system of combining medical school with hands-on hospital and patient experience. In most states at the time, medical students took only two four-month courses to earn a diploma and license to practice. To graduate from LICH, students took the two required courses but also had to be twenty-one years of age. Dickinson, who finished first in his class at age twenty, had to wait to graduate with the class of 1882. The year's delay caused a turning point in his professional life, for in addition to interning at Williamsburg Hospital, he assisted one of his former professors, Alexander Skene, a prominent gynecologist and scholar. This relationship led to Dickinson's close involvement for most of the 1880s in the writing of Skene's highly regarded book, *Treatise on the Diseases of Women*. Of the book's 161 illustrations, Dickinson drew 105 of them. Work on Skene's book over this decade meant that Dickinson had less time for his own research and writing, although he did publish articles, including an important one on the anatomical harm to women who wore hour-glass corsets. He also wrote articles on how to improve office efficiency and hospital administration. In time, his gift for organization led to his becoming an active member on local and national boards in the medical field. His renown in this area also resulted in his appointment to the Council of National Defense's Medical Board in Washington, DC, during World War I.

Before his official graduation from medical school, Dickinson accepted an appointment as "police surgeon" for Brooklyn's nascent municipal civil service. In this capacity he handled much tenement-house work, out of which he developed the foundation for his own private practice. Delivering babies in the tenements, where risk of infection was high, Dickinson tied off the umbilical cord with sterilized thread before cutting it with scissors, which subsequently became standard medical practice. Always ready with a quip, Dickinson once said that his new way of handling the umbilical cord was his most significant contribution to medicine "since it is the one and only act of surgical interference each human being in the civilized world undergoes."[4]

By this time, the Dickinson family lived in Brooklyn Heights at 159 Clinton Street, and the ground floor, which had a separate entrance just below street level, became the young practitioner's office. "In those days, no woman would go into an office building. She had to go into a house—any patient must, particularly a woman. So we converted the ground floor into a waiting room, and my parents lived on the upper three floors," Dickinson later told his family.[5] In 1886, Dickinson began lecturing in obstetrics at LICH, and remained on the staff until retirement. He also worked at the Kings County, Methodist, and Brooklyn hospitals and was known for being one of New York's top medical teachers.

Family and Nature

Toward the end of the 1880s, Dickinson met Sarah Truslow (1863–1938) and fell in love. She came from an educated, well-to-do family and had graduated from Brooklyn's Packer Institute. Along with a friend, Emily Wood, she started Brooklyn's Young Women's Christian Association (YWCA), where she organized programs and led a well-attended Bible class. Later on, she organized the national YWCA and also helped international branches start up. She was instrumental to the founding of other important organizations, including the Brooklyn Auxiliary of the New York Committee of Fourteen, dedicated to combating commercialized vice and the white slave trade, and the Travelers Aid Society, for visitors and newcomers to the city. Even before the couple's eighteen-month engagement, Dickinson wrote daily to his beloved. According to an unpublished biography of Dickinson, written by his son-in-law George Barbour, many of the love letters were "embellished with black or colored decorations—marginal sketches of places or things seen during the day, thumbnail vignettes of people he had met, sprays of flowers in delicate tints, initial capitals with medieval serifs, elaborate scrollwork and the like."[6] While Sarah was an unusually serious woman who had considered a missionary life to better serve God, Dickinson, a liberal Episcopalian, had a lighter, sociable side and a ready sense of humor. His many letters to Sarah during their courtship reveal the dominant themes in his life, "the steady, hard pace of the day's work, his devotion to his calling, his human sympathy, his love of the out-of-doors and beauty in nature, solicitousness for [Sarah's] health, and longing to find approval in her sight."[7]

They married on May 7, 1890, in the Truslow home, and rented a house at 145 Clinton Street in Brooklyn. Later the couple bought a home at 168 Clinton Street, where they remained until the end of the First World War, when they decided to move permanently to Manhattan. Their first daughter, Margaret, was born prematurely and died. A second daughter, Dorothy, was born in August 1892, and another daughter, Jean, in July 1896. The Dickinson household included both the family home and a busy doctor's office. Household help allowed both parents to pursue their careers. Although Dickinson's growing clientele drew predominantly from the educated classes, he provided services to untold numbers who could not afford to pay, and most of his voluminous case histories came from this charity work.

Dickinson's idealism, activism, and achievements in the medical profession deserve a full-length biography. Glimpses of his personal life reveal his joy in nature, which was the inspiration for his landscape drawings. His many letters to Sarah over the years showed this side of him. In the summer of 1893, he wrote to her from Watermill, Long Island:

> What wonderful things the Great Artist can do with the least of means! With mountains and lakes, or cliffs and heavy surf, one expects grandeur and power—with trees and meadows, brooks, flowers and animal life, one looks for the beauty of tender drawing and color—but given a simple sky without a cloud, an unbroken stretch of blue water, and a strip of yellow beach, He can show either the power or the tenderness. Have you ever burst out on Shinnecock Hills on a clear summer day, after hours in the scrub pines and the dust? It was the smile of the Lord, a glory, a wonder.[8]

Dickinson's family remembered how often he would stop to take in a breath-taking view or a simple stand of trees and say, "Glory to God!"[9] Toward the end of his life, he told his family what constituted the "sight of sights in America"— a boat ride through Champlain and the Hudson in pursuit of autumn's red maples. "We went up to the upper part of the White Mountains and we saw the glory of God there, and then we came down by the Catskills and Mohonk, and I've got color sketches to prove it. We saw the very glory of God, and were off and free, and away from the telephone."[10]

Dickinson's courtship drawing probably portrays himself and Sarah Truslow. From the Robert Latou Dickinson Papers, 1861–1950 (B MS c72), Boston Medical Library in the Francis A. Countway Library of Medicine.

Dickinson often escaped the city's frenzy to enjoy nature's serenity. He thrived in both worlds, but the latter served his spirit. Of his fondness for biking he wrote to Sarah, "Truly, the wheel makes the park our front yard, and puts All Outdoors just beyond. We wheelmen own the Earth. One can talk, as one can't in a rattling wagon…and there's health and exhilaration, and sweet temper and patience."[11] On another occasion he wrote her:

From four to seven I rode thirty miles, discovering paths in woods long coveted, now owned. This was a day of Chasing Clouds and Cloud Shadows. A not distant wood, so overhung, was intense blue-black. Nearer, all the trees in clear spring greens still. Potato fields were at their best, level, solid color not yet dimmed. The young corn was level and unbroken color too, and toward the west reflecting light, as though the shining leaves were rippling water. Clover and honeysuckle scent filled the air, till the salt marsh was reached. Between the Red Hill and Sheepshead Bay are three long wooded points, uninhabited, reaching out into the salt meadows— cedars chiefly, so tangled with vines that one may not see ten feet, rank and overgrown. Paths only, or wood roads.[12]

Nature inspired him. Fortunately, he had a creative outlet for the soaring emotions natural landscapes stirred in him, and the drawings he made enriched, and continue to enrich, other people's lives by voicing a joy in life with which many people identify but which they are are less able to express artistically. From a sailing trip in 1899, Dickinson wrote to Sarah:

In a blaze and glare of light such as I like, we are cutting along on one long reach from Fisher's Island to Shelter Island….After a dip this morning and a spun-out breakfast, we tramped about Fisher's Island, seeing fine swales, inlets, and cottages, on a bare rolling island shore, without trees, but with strong thick bushes in the hollows.
    This is life to me. And with all the long and lazy hours, the fact there has been and will be work to do, and the constant motion of the boat gives a sense of activity, of outdoor life, only matched, if at all, in camp…. Can you feel the sun soak you through and through, and the wind blow cool? Do your ears ever lose the music of the ripple against a boat, or your eyes the glint along the water, or the shine under dark and overhanging shores?[13]

The Medical Man

In an insightful discussion of Dickinson's complex contribution to twentieth-century medicine, and in particular to the contraception movement, historian James Reed remarks on Dickinson's naturalist approach as a clinical practitioner, which was undoubtedly influenced by his innate Thoreauvian eye for detail and record-keeping: "[S]tretching over forty years, [Dickinson's] records were a medical natural history and the essential source on which he drew in founding American medical sex research."[14] Lura Beam, his collaborator in synthesizing his 5,200 case histories on his patients, wrote of his gift for observation and data collecting:

> He noted background, history of the symptoms, diagnosis and treatment, recording fluctuations visit by visit as long as the women remained in his care.... The doctor was an astute observer and an expert listener. The patients' posture, manner, expression and even his reticence were evidence. Her body spoke to him, in its entirety.[15]

When Dickinson embarked on the research phase of his career in the 1920s, Reed points out that he had "no training in basic science. He had devoted his life to 'the study of womankind,' and like all great naturalists, he knew what could be discovered by the naked eye about his subject."[16] Reed also compares Dickinson's personalized religion to "the nature celebration of John Burroughs."[17] Connecting Dickinson's medical practice and overall approach to life to the intrinsic qualities of a naturalist can also apply to his artistic output and probably stands as his most distinguishing characteristic in life. That is, his naturalist's eye fueled his productivity in a variety of undertakings. This pronounced quality, along with his friendly spirit and empathy, brought him widespread admiration and success.

In the first phase of Dickinson's career—that of clinical practitioner—he pioneered a new level of the doctor and female patient relationship. His social beliefs and ideals, along with a sense of noblesse oblige, influenced his style of medical practice. One of his deeply held tenets was the possibility of happy marriage, which proper sex education, premarital care, and marriage counseling could help ensure. In a 1907 talk on marital maladjustment he said that "no single cause of mental strain in married women is as wide spread as sex fears and maladjustments," and that "in most divorces the initial source of friction lies in a real or fancied physical incompatibility." Dickinson advocated that it was the physician's duty to provide sex counseling "to save his people from their ignorance."[18] Offering information on birth control contributed significantly to sexual adjustment, the key to marital happiness. Thus Dickinson pioneered a close doctor-patient relationship at a time when many gynecologists avoided physical examinations of unmarried women altogether. As Reed points out, "Dickinson's lasting contributions to his specialty were made possible by his willingness to discuss sex with his patients and to base treatment not upon an abstract code of properties but upon the needs revealed by pelvic examination."[19]

Dickinson was a leading Progressive Era doctor who, over the course of his career, became the strongest force in changing attitudes within the conservative medical profession relative to sexual reform. He argued that marriage was not merely for procreation, but for the unique relationship between husband and wife; sex was to be enjoyed as an end in itself, and when couples had better sexual adjustment (i.e., knowledge of and access to contraception), a richer relationship followed. Dickinson countered arguments that contraception was a violation of nature by saying that "the natural order was good [but] could be and should be improved by human agents."[20] His eminence, affability, humor, and diplomacy made even his most challenging medical opponents acquiesce in the end. He was seen as a Christian gentleman and orthodox physician in contrast to such "radicals" as birth-control activist Margaret Sanger (1879–1966), who held similar views.

By the 1920s, Dickinson's meticulous and pioneering record-keeping on patients amounted to not only thousands of illustrated case histories but also 1,200 sex histories, which formed the foundation for the second phase of his career in sex research, publications, and lobbying for acceptance of birth control clinics by the American Medical Association. From 1923 to about 1940, Dickinson's indefatigable activity focused mainly on the Committee on Maternal Health (CMH), which he founded initially to carry out medical investigation of contraception and related issues, although its role evolved. He put doctors who opposed his views on the committee, because he wanted the organization to represent medical opinion, and it did. His opponents cooperated because they wanted "to keep contraception under strict medical control" and out of the hands of the lay radicals.[21]

Dickinson's new focus on sex research and lobbying led to collaboration with Margaret Sanger. Years before he had politely refused her request for support, but during the somewhat turbulent years of steering his Committee on Maternal Health, he found that he needed her group—the Clinical Research Bureau (CRB)—for its data on contraceptive patients, and her clinic needed his first-rate medical supervision and endorsement. Although Dickinson readily accepted the opportunity to take over Sanger's clinic, which would provide him the research results he needed, legal obstacles prevented licensing of their proposed Maternity Research Council. Thus in 1930, Dickinson joined Sanger's

CRB as an individual and not as a joint partner with his Committee of Maternal Health.

Although Dickinson and Sanger had differences of opinion at times, they grew closer over their years of collaboration toward to the same goal of improving women's lives by making contraception safely available to them. In the late 1930s, Dickinson came to Sanger's defense when new leaders of the American Birth Control League criticized her:

> Mrs. Sanger is the symbol, the international figure, possessed of ability to beget enthusiasm for this work beyond anyone else whatever…. She has a way of delivering the goods which makes our other groups appear somewhat as though mechanisms of organization, conformities…and fear of the medical guild were their main concern."[22]

Still later, Dickinson designed the medallion for Planned Parenthood Federation of America, which became the Lasker Award; he was its first recipient.

Dickinson made medical history by being the invincible bridge between the birth control movement and organized medicine. When obtaining clinical data from hospitals failed as a means to changing the medical profession's attitude toward contraception, his Committee on Maternal Health changed tactics and became a clearinghouse for information, publishing scholarly monographs that served as physician handbooks on a variety of sexual topics. The goal was "to furnish every doctor knowledge and courage that he may give to every patient information and comfort concerning the contraceptive best suited for her proven needs." After Louise Stevens Bryant joined the CMH staff as executive secretary in late 1926, the committee entered its most productive period, and soon voted "to divert all resources to publication." Bryant had a Ph.D. from the University of Pennsylvania in medical science and played a key role in the committee's numerous and important publications, including her coauthorship of the widely circulated and standard-setting Control of Contraception (1931). Dickinson's seminal collaborations with author Lura Beam also played a role in the American Medical Association's official acceptance of contraception.[23]

Dickinson's relentless and high-spirited efforts to educate the public on matters related to reproduction and the goal of improving women's lives included collaborating with sculptor Abram Belskie in the late 1930s on twenty-four life-size sculptures depicting the birth process. This series, now housed in the Cleveland Art Museum of Health, led to a published version titled Birth Atlas. Each sculpture shows one stage in the reproductory cycle: fertilization, fetal development, labor, and birth. More than two million people viewed these sculptures at the 1939 World's Fair, "probably the most successful single effort at sex education ever staged." In true Dickinsonian form, "getting the word out" was a vital and essential hands-on experience that the master teacher thoroughly enjoyed, as told by an affectionate witness:

> In the days when the New York World's Fair was being built, Dr. Dickinson [about age seventy-five] often carried his sculptures out to Flushing Meadows on the BMT subway. He would sit in a corner of the subway car and then with a pixie-like gleam in his eyes, slowly unwrap the birth model. Soon his blasé neighbors in the car would take notice. Some would begin to ask questions. Then a crowd would collect and he would begin a public lecture on human reproduction.[24]

One of his associates later wrote of the sculptures, "In all these works, he wedded art with science, and beauty with strict accuracy."[25]

When he died at age eighty-nine following complications related to prostate cancer, Dickinson was embarking on his "third career" of medical and autobiographical writing, even though he could rest assured that his first and second careers had already caused important shifts in social attitudes that affected the quality of life for women, and in turn, for families. His ideals, beliefs, acumen, and creativity propelled him into life works that deserve further study. Indeed it can be said that "Although Dickinson did not live to see the end of 'The Age of Hush and Pretend,' he had initiated the process of preparing his profession to deal with the sexual needs of modern America."[26]

Dickinson's Washington Years

The United States' involvement in World War I created an interlude between Dickinson's two career phases in medicine. During those years, 1917 to 1919, Dickinson served the war effort in Washington, DC, and immediately afterward traveled as a government Public Health Service representative to China, Japan, and Korea. From these years of travel he left behind sketchbooks, including one rare binder of Washington's landscapes, the focus of this volume.

Dickinson came to Washington in the fall of 1917 to serve on the newly established General Medical Board of the Army's Council of National Defense, chaired by Dr. Franklin Martin, secretary general of the American College of Surgeons. The board rapidly grew in size from thirty-five to one hundred distinguished doctors. Until the Armistice of November 1918, the medical section—organized into numerous committees—steered a vast war-mobilization network involving medical resources in relation to state and municipal activities, legislation, sanitation, research, hospitals, nurses, volunteer women, and training. The Medical Board met on Sunday mornings in a forum "brimming with interest" that included Allied representatives assigned to Washington

Robert L. Dickinson in his army uniform, Washington, DC, ca. 1917, age fifty-six. Robert Latou Dickinson Papers, 1861–1950 (B MS c72), Boston Medical Library in the Francis A. Countway Library of Medicine.

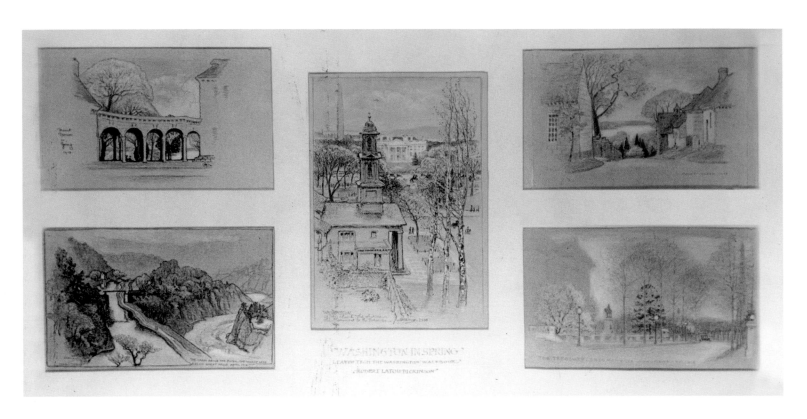

Dickinson's Washington sketches on an album page in his papers. Robert Latou Dickinson Papers, 1861–1950 (B MS c72), Boston Medical Library in the Francis A. Countway Library of Medicine.

commissions. Dickinson served on the board's Volunteer Medical Service Corps and the Committee of Medical Advisory Boards.[27] His army salary was $4,250 a year, prompting him to write his wife in a letter, "No wonder the generals and colonels of the Reg. Army wear shiny ancient clothes, even when in high places here."[28]

True to his reputation that led to his Washington appointment, Dickinson ran an active office, as described by one of his assistants, who also noted his affinity for the outdoors:

> During these years it seemed as if Dr. Dickinson had his finger in every pie that was being baked. The most distinguished men in many fields came to his office. Surgeon Gen'l Gorgas, the Mayo brothers, Paul Manship, dropped in constantly. It was my business to type and file the notes he took during important conferences. Many times the margins of these papers would be covered with cartoons or caricatures of the members of the committee.... It was fun taking care of such a dynamic personality but a task impossible to do single-handed. Between your mother and me, we managed to do a pretty good job and a daily phone call would keep things in order.... Occasionally no one could find him anywhere but in due course, he would return to the office looking fit as a fiddle, greatly invigorated by a swim in the muddy Potomac."[29]

Dickinson lived temporarily at the Cosmos Club until he found an apartment on an upscale block of K Street near Fourteenth Street (see page 103). Sarah visited several times, but for the most part Dickinson was alone in Washington and wrote Sarah frequently about his demanding work life and the solace and refreshment he found in Washington's beautiful surroundings. His excursions along the Potomac River soon inspired plans for a "Washington Walk Book." One letter to Sarah mentions having a car for "fine drives" along the Potomac, and a later one describes a canoe trip to Trammel's inn, sixteen miles north of the city, where in August 1918 it was "cool enough for a big fire on the rocks." With youthful zest Dickinson declares, "An entirely new section of the river is conquered. Next week...onward to Seneca and Pennyfield Lock to be done the following week."[30] (Dickinson's sketches of Trammel's and Pennyfield Lock and scenes near his residence appear in chapters two and three.)

As Dickinson's outdoor Potomac adventures advanced, he sought an appropriate map, which he eventually created himself, with the initial help of the U.S. Geological Survey. He wrote to Sarah:

> While in the Geological Survey about some hospital-location maps, seeing the aviation birdseye views—the roll reaching from W[ashington] to N.Y. that unfolds before the postal aviator—I asked if they had the Potomac, to illustrate walks about W[ashington]. "No, but I'll send a machine up the river to get the whole roll for you, as far as you want." What ho! What's the matter with living among mainsprings?[31]

A remarkable, original map resulted and has been reproduced for this book. Measuring approximately nineteen by twenty-three inches, the map was drawn on vellum, the standard material of the day used by surveyors and craftsmen. Vellum, a durable, variable-weather paper, has a coated surface that holds ink. Its transparency made it easy to photostat, a popular means of reproducing printed matter in Dickinson's day.[32]

Dickinson based his Potomac map on two U.S. Geological Survey maps, one from 1910 and one from 1915. During the research for this book, a photostatted copy of a second Dickinson map turned up at the Sycamore Island Canoe Club, near Glen Echo. This second map bears a number in the bottom right corner, which could be a plate number, but no trace of the original could be found. Dickinson's calligraphy in the upper right corner of the second map tells us that it is a "sketch map in its first attempt," in other words, the draft version for his final map included at the back of this volume. The final map, for instance, omits the trolley schedule to Great Falls.

Dickinson's map proved a valuable resource for this book, as it identifies the location of many of his drawings and includes annotations about some of them, such as Prospect Rock, a Potomac wonder of the world no longer accessible to hikers. The map tells us about recreational life along the Potomac in the early twentieth century, information not found in local history books. The map stands as a significant cultural and historical resource on Washington, DC.

During Dickinson's eighteen-month tour of duty in Washington, he dearly missed his wife Sarah. In a letter from November 1918, he laments, "When you are here, O Completeness, I am Head-man and Heart-man. When you are away and the heart has gone out of this town, then only head work remains."[33] His letters counsel her to take care of her health and avoid stress, and one, in particular, urges her to follow his own prescription for handling intense work life, which is to get outdoors:

> Observe me…. No working holidays…. Off two and a half days. One lazy, one vigorous, one lazy. All along the river that is café au lait with milk in color, but stained right for the boys in khaki therefore. The soldiers we meet are so agape at officers with packs and rolled up sleeves and flannel shirts under service hats they forget to salute. We meet no other officer hikers, we do find keen interest in a trail book, and many to con our maps.[34]

As Dickinson's idea for a Washington Walk Book developed, he embarked on excursions to other landmarks in and around Washington, such as Arlington Cemetery, Mount Vernon, St. Paul's Church, and Fairfax Courthouse. Likely Dickinson was following the guidelines for his New York Walk Book, which included tours of both Manhattan and its outskirts. As mentioned earlier, his Washington research led him to meet the area's leading walking historian "The Rambler," who from 1912–1926 wrote columns for the *Evening Star* about his treks and the families he met along the way. J. Harry Shannon (1869–1928), the *Star*'s "Rambler," was a few years younger than Dickinson and from the existing evidence accompanied him to Prospect Rock (see pages 50–51).

Shannon certainly would have been the best resource at the time for Dickinson's Walk Book, for he knew his way on foot to all the locations Dickinson drew and could offer history and anecdotes for many of them. Portions of several Rambler articles are reproduced in this volume, in part to record Shannon's contribution to an era of Washington's history.[35]

Dickinson's Washington drawings left to the Library of Congress in 1941 remain in his original three-ring binder. The sketches were done on medium-weight, wove gray paper and cream-colored drawing paper. Dickinson worked in pen and ink, fountain pen, pastels, charcoal, graphite pencil, colored pencils, and white chalk. He glued the drawings onto sheets of paper and penciled notations on size in the margins. The final printed illustrations were to be almost thumbnails, as his goal was a portable guidebook. The trim size of his original *New York Walk Book* was 5½ by 7½ inches, and its drawings compare in size to those planned for the Washington Walk Book. Many of the drawings in the binder were protected with an overlaying page that is now brittle and discolored.[36]

Dickinson began drawing from early childhood but never pursued formal art training. He learned from observation and incorporated a variety of styles into his work, including those of contemporary artists whose studios he visited. As a thirty-five-year-old in 1895, he visited Arthur Dow's studio at the Pratt Institute in New York and acquired an interest in Japanese art. Thereafter, prints by Hokusai and Hiroshige hung in his home. In this volume, "Tossing Water," on page 19, shows the influence Hokusai had on Dickinson. He also designed and had built an authentic Japanese summerhouse on Westhampton Beach, Long Island, which unfortunately burned down.[37] His home bookshelves included many calligraphy texts, and his archived papers demonstrate that he experimented with calligraphy on a daily basis. Throughout his life, Dickinson pursued and created art and once said of himself, "I am twins—a surgeon and an artist. Sometimes I don't know which it is that I am."[38]

Most of Dickinson's Washington landscapes have a sweet quality. They invite the viewer to join the enchanted world inside the image. Trees often frame his settings, serving as gateways to nature's sublime wonder. Tiny figures populate his magical realms. They stand on a distant bridge, canoe down the river, camp, play, or enjoy a romantic moment. People, birds, and small animals share nature's glory together, an idea close to Dickinson's heart and spiritual beliefs.

Dickinson's scenic drawings are important for their charm, their message, and their documentation of Washington, DC, in the second decade of the twentieth century. For Washingtonians and visitors today, they also reiterate the unique beauty and value of the Potomac River and its surroundings. Just miles from the nation's urban capital lie a wondrous river gorge, hundreds of tributary streams, woods, trails, vistas, bike paths, and undulating countryside. The physical beauty of Washington is not static but alive, attracting visitors and outdoor enthusiasts in every season. While river camps for fishing and canoeing were popular destinations in Dickinson's day, other forms of recreation dominate today—kayaking, biking, hiking, and birding. Dickinson's sketches remind us that outdoor life has always been part of living in Washington. His inspiration for the natural beauty he discovered while on duty in Washington becomes our inspiration today, to maintain these places, to cherish and preserve them.

Although the current volume is not the trail book or tour guide Dickinson might have imagined, it attempts to reach audiences with the doctor-artist's joy in nature, which his own words in a letter to his wife best capture:

> Would that you could see this winter color—the white ice, the black water, the long yellow shoreline under the purple horizon of hills, all beneath the clearest of skies. How the hillsides have filled me with gladness!…You would hold your breath to see it![39]

Endnotes

Endnotes

1 *Great Falls and the C&O Canal*

1. For readers interested in detailed geologic information, the U.S. Geological Survey has posted online its famous booklet *The River and the Rocks* (USGS Bulletin 1471): http://www.nps.gov/history/history/online_books/geology/books-geology.htm/. See also Albert Atwood, "Potomac River Destiny," *National Geographic Magazine*, July 1945: 70; and Mike High, *The C&O Canal Companion* (Baltimore: Johns Hopkins University Press, 2000), 238–42. Quotation from: http://www.nps.gov/gwmp/index.htm. For those seeking more information on early land grant history pertaining to the Potomac's source, Mike High's detailed *C&O Canal Companion* Web site offers much history and provides bibliographic references: see www.press.jhu.edu/press/books/potomac-canal.htm. Local birding information can be found in Claudia Wilds, *Finding Birds in the National Capital Area* (Washington: Smithsonian Institution Press, 1992). The Maryland Ornithological Society has a wealth of birding information on its Web site: http://www.mdbirds.org.

2. Quotation from http://www.press.jhu.edu/books/supplemental/canal/smithatlittlefalls.html. The site, related to High's *C&O Canal Companion*, posts the John Smith quote with the following source information: "This transcription is found in *The Travels and Works of John Smith* (Volume 1), edited by Edward Arbor and A.G. Bradley. A more modern (and superbly annotated) presentation of Smith's works is found in the three volume *Complete Works of Captain John Smith*, edited by Philip Barbour, published in 1986 by the University of North Carolina Press and the Institute for American History and Culture (Williamsburg, Virginia)."

3. High, *C&O Canal Companion*, 1–9.

4. Audubon Society of the District of Columbia, *The Potomac Valley: History and Prospect* (Washington: Audubon Society of the District of Columbia, 1952).

5. Frederick Tilp, *This Was Potomac River* (Alexandria, Va.: Frederick Tilp, 1978), 188–93.

6. Ibid.

7. Wilbur E. Garrett, "The Patowmack Canal: Waterway That Led to the Constitution," *National Geographic* 171:6 (June 1987), 731.

8. Tilp, *Potomac River*, 305.

9. Ibid., 306.

10. Ibid., 306–7.

11. Mary Louise Shafter, "Recreation in Arlington County, 1870–1920," *Arlington Historical Magazine* 6:2 (October 1978), 62.

12. Joel Achenbach, "Potomac Dreaming," *Washington Post Magazine*, May 5, 2002, 20–21.

13. Albert W. Atwood, "Potomac River Destiny," *National Geographic Magazine*, July 1945, 40; Garrett, "Patowmack Canal," 725.

14. Garrett, "Patowmack Canal," 744.

15. Atwood, "River of Destiny," 49.

16. Garrett, "Patowmack Canal," 730–31; Barry Mackintosh, *C&O Canal: The Making of a Park* (Washington: U.S. Department of the Interior, National Park Service, 1991), 2.

17. Frederick Doering, "Potomac Almanac, History of Potomac," manuscript, 1970, C&O Canal Library, Hagerstown, Md.

18. Ibid.

19. Elizabeth Kytle, *Time Was: A Cabin John Memory Book: Interviews with 18 Old-Timers* (Cabin John, Md.: Cabin John Citizens' Association, 1976), 6.

20. E-mail from Rod Sauter, Supervisory Park Ranger, C&O Canal, National Historic Park, National Park Service, February 22, 2005; e-mail from Mike High (author of *The C&O Canal Companion*), April 11, 2006.

21. Kytle, *Cabin John*, 9.

22. Thomas F. "Swiftwater" Hahn, *The Chesapeake and Ohio Canal Lock-Houses & Lock-Keepers* (Morgantown: Institute for the History of Technology and Industrial Archaeology at West Virginia University, 1996).

23. Kytle, *Cabin John*, 13–14.

24. High, *C&O Canal Companion*, 41.

25. Ibid., 43.

26. Ibid., 44. Information on the canal's 1844 and 1878 mortgages came from an undated National Park Service manuscript by Walter S. Sanderlin, "A Study of the History of the Potomac River Valley," 128; another Sanderlin source later called to the author's attention is *The Great National Project* (Baltimore: Johns Hopkins University Press, 1946).

27. Mackintosh, *C&O Canal*, 2–3.

28. Ibid., 96.

29. Ibid., 18–19, 31, 46.

30. Ibid., 44.

31. *Washington Post*, January 19, 1954.

32. High, *C&O Canal Companion*, 47–48.

33. Thomas F. "Swiftwater" Hahn, *Towpath Guide to the C&O Canal* (Shepherdstown, W.Va.: American Canal and Transportation Center, 1982; reprint, 1990), 44–46; National Park Service, "Great Falls Tavern," information sheet (Hagerstown, Md.: U.S. Department of the Interior, National Park Service, Chesapeake and Ohio Canal National Historical Park, October 2002).

34. Jim Fearson, "Chain Bridge: A History of the Bridge and Its Surrounding Territory, 1608–1991," *Arlington Historical Magazine* 9 (October 1991), 8–9. The Rambler quote, on page 42, is from Fearson's article, page 16.

35. Ibid., 8–9; 20.

36. Ibid., 11.

37. Ibid., 13–14.

38. Elizabeth Miles Cooke, *The History of the Georgetown Pike* (Annandale, Va.: Elizabeth Miles Cooke and Charles Baptie Studios, 1977).

39. Marty Smith, "How Does Scott's Run?" Article posted at www. fairfaxcounty.gov/parks/resources/archives/scottsrun.htm.

40. Ibid.

41. Ibid.

42. Cooke, *Georgetown Pike*; Phil Hill et al., "The Burling Tract Conflict," *Essay Awards, Historical Society of Fairfax County, Va.*, vol. 1 (1983); Conversations with Jim Olmsted, McLean, Va., September 2003.

43. Smith, "How Does Scott Run?"

2   River Camps and Cabin John

1. J. R. Hildebrand, "The Sources of Washington's Charm," *National Geographic Magazine*, June 1923, 671.

2. Ibid.

3. Dusty Rhodes, interview with the author, November 16, 2004; Gilbert Grosvenor, "The Great Falls of the Potomac," *National Geographic Magazine*, March 1928, 396.

4. Grosvenor, "The Great Falls of the Potomac," 396.

5. Mackintosh, *C&O Canal*.

6. Mike High, *The C&O Canal Companion* (Baltimore: Johns Hopkins University Press, 2000), 134.

7. Hahn, *Towpath Guide*, 54.

8. "Potomac Almanac, History of Potomac," manuscript, 1970, C&O Canal Library, Hagerstown, Md.

9. J. H. Wilson Marriott, "Picturesque Cabin John, a Bit of History," manuscript, 1903, 1, vertical files, Montgomery County Historical Society, Rockville, Md.

10. Edith Martin Armstrong, "A Brief History of Cabin John Park," manuscript, 1947, 4, vertical files, Montgomery County Historical Society.

11. Marriott, "Picturesque Cabin John," 5.

12. Armstrong, "A Brief History," 3.

13. Untitled clipping, *Evening Star*, April 6, 1913, vertical files, Montgomery County Historical Society.

14. J. Yowell, "The Cabin of John" (undated brochure), The Historical Society of Washington, DC.

15. Marriot, "Picturesque Cabin John."

16. *Evening Star*, April 6, 1913.

17. Ibid.

18. D. D. Gaillard, "The Washington Aqueduct and Cabin John Bridge," *National Geographic Magazine*, December 1897, 344; see also http://allenbrowne.blogspot.com/2011/05/cabin-john-bridge.html for interesting images.

19. Ibid.; untitled clipping, *M/Gazette*, July 24, 1998, vertical files, Montgomery County Historical Society.

20. Armstrong, "A Brief History," 7.

21. Kytle, *Cabin John*, 50–55.

22. Ibid., 53.

23. Ibid., 57.

24. Ibid., 59.

25. Burr Gray, president, Cabin John Citizens' Association, interview with the author, January 2004.

26. Richard Cook and Deborah Lange, *Glen Echo Park: A Story of Survival, Glen Echo* (Bethesda, Md.: Bethesda Communications Group, 2000), 14–16.

27. Ibid., 27.

28. Ibid., 73–74.

29. Ibid., 95.

30. U.S. Department of the Interior, National Park Service, *Clara Barton* (Washington: U.S. Department of the Interior, 1981), 35.

31. Ibid., 36.

32. Ibid., 50.

33. Ibid., 58–59.

34. Ibid., 64.

3 *Washington Landmarks*

1. Information for this entry was taken from the National Park Service's Web site: www.nps.gov/cherry/index.htm and from Paul Russell, "Japanese Spring in America," Asia 30 (May 1930). The quotes by Louis J. Halle are from *Spring in Washington* (New York: William Sloane Association, 1947), 47, 55–56.

2. George Thomas Kurian, ed., *A Historical Guide to the U.S. Government* (New York: Oxford University Press, 1998), 531; Heritage Cavaliers, *The Nation's Capital* (Washington: Heritage Cavaliers, 1967), 67–69.

3. Information from Dr. Pamela Henson, Historian, Smithsonian Archives, Smithsonian Institution, 2005.

4. Kurian, *Historical Guide*, 532.

5. Information for this entry came from several sources: Historic American Buildings Survey, HABS no. DC-673, Prints and Photographs Division, Library of Congress; Harriet Riddle Davis, "Civil War Recollections of a Little Yankee," *Records of the Columbia Historical Society*, 1944, 55–69; George Olszewski, *Franklin Park* (Washington: Division of History, Office of Archaeology and Historic Preservation, 1970); and Tanya Edward Beauchamp, e-mail to the author, May 10, 2006. The Franklin School became a National Historic Landmark in 1996, with a Historic Structure Report from July 1994 describing it; the report includes information on the park.

6. "The Fiftieth Anniversary of the U.S. Department of Justice Building," manuscript, 1984, U.S. Department of Justice Library; U.S. Department of Justice, brochure, (Washington: U.S. Department of Justice, 1998); http://www.fbi.gov. John Fox, FBI historian, interview with the author, August 3, 2005; U.S. Department of Justice, Federal Bureau of Investigation, "Principal Offices of the FBI—Past and Present," manuscript, undated.

7. Information on the church came from the following sources: Bryan G. Hayden, interview with the author, February 2004; Constance McLaughlin Green, *The Church on Lafayette Square, 1815–1970* (Washington: Potomac Books, 1970); Alexander Hagner, "History and Reminiscences of St. John's Church, Washington, DC," *Records of the Columbia Historical Society*, 1908.

8. Edith Schafer, *Aspects of Georgetown* (Washington: Flaneur Press, 2004).

9. Kathryn Schneider Smith, ed., *Washington at Home: An Illustrated History of Neighborhoods in the Nation's Capital* (Eugene, Ore.: Windsor Publications, 1988), 25, 22. Other sources include Heritage Cavaliers, *The Nation's Capital*, 210–25; D. Randolph Keim, *Keim's Illustrated Handbook: Washington and Its Environs* (Washington: published privately, 1874); Francis E. Leupp, *Walks about Washington*, with drawings by Lester G. Hornby (Boston: Little Brown, 1915); and http://en.wikipedia.org/wiki/Georgetown_(Washington,_D.C.); Ray Kukulski and Bill Gallagher, "Washington's Trolley System: The Forces That Shaped It, the Benefits That Were Created, and the Elements That Caused Its Demise," a presentation, March 7, 2009.

10. For more information on saving the canal and parkland see: www.savethecanal.org.

11. Jack Spratt, "Rock Creek's Bridges," *Records of the Columbia Historical Society*, 1953–1956, 63; Donald Myer, *Bridges and the City of Washington* (Washington: Commission of Fine Arts, 1974), 68. See also http://en.wikipedia.org/wiki/Taft_Bridge, consulted on August 20, 2007; "Tank and Airplane in Day of Thrills," *Evening Star*, April 20, 1918; and "Success of Liberty Day Capital's Aim," *Evening Star*, April 23, 1918.

12. Gail Spilsbury, *Rock Creek Park* (Baltimore: Johns Hopkins University Press), 2002.

13. Ibid., 45.

14. Research for this enty came from *The Adams Memorial*, pamphlet (Washington: Rock Creek Cemetery, 1997), and a church booklet, *Two Hundred Twenty-Fifth Anniversary, St. Paul's Episcopal Church* (Washington: Rock Creek Parish, 1944).

15. Matthew Pinsker, *Lincoln's Sanctuary: Abraham Lincoln and the Soldiers' Home* (Oxford and New York: Oxford University Press, 2003), 1–17; www.lincolncottage.org; www.afrhdevelopment.com.

16. Paul R. Goode, *The United States Soldiers' Home* (Richmond, Va.: William Byrd Press, 1957), 42; the Anderson Cottage name is described in an Armed Forces Retirement Home (AFRH) handout, "Historic Buildings at the U.S. Soldiers' and Airmen's Home."

17. Pinsker, *Lincoln's Sanctuary*, 163.

18. Pinsker, *Lincoln's Sanctuary*, 140; Goode, *Soldiers' Home*, 80.

19. Goode, *Soldiers' Home*, 3–9.

20. See http://www.afrh.gov.

21. Goode, *Soldiers' Home*, 3.

22. Goode, *Soldiers' Home*, appendix D.

23. Shelia Abarr, e-mail to the author, November 17, 2003; updated information from Chris Black, December 15, 2005.

24. Goode, *Soldiers' Home*, 204; Chris Black, e-mail to the author, May 9, 2006, on the AFRH's land loss.

4 Maryland and Virginia Sites

1. "The Rambler," *Evening Star*, May 14, 1916.

2. "Helen Powell, In Her Own Words," *Prince George's Exeter*, January 27, 1999.

3. Eleonor M. V. Cook, "A History of Early Water Mills in Montgomery County, Maryland," manuscript, 1990, Montgomery County Historical Society, Rockville, Md., 112. The quotation from Theodore Roosevelt's letter to his son is from Joseph B. Bishop, *Theodore Roosevelt's Letters to His Children* (New York: New American Library of World Literature, 1964), 70.

4. Ibid.

5. Quotations from Washington's writings are from Joanne Young and Taylor Biggs Lewis Jr., *Washington's Mount Vernon* (New York: Holt, Rinehart and Winston, 1973), unnumbered page (April 16, 1785), and Worth E. Shoults, "The Home of the First Farmer of America," *National Geographic Magazine*, May 1928, 603.

6. Gerald Johnson *Mount Vernon: The Story of a Shrine*, with epilogue by Ellen McCallister (Mount Vernon, Va.: Mount Vernon Ladies' Association, 2002), 61. See also Mac Griswold, *Washington's Gardens at Mount Vernon* (Boston: Houghton, Mifflin Company, 1999). Griswold's illustrated history of Mount Vernon's gardens includes detailed plant appendixes: "George Washington's Trees and Shrubs"; "Eighteenth-Century Flowers;" "Bulbs Grown Today at Mount Vernon"; "Old Roses Grown Today at Mount Vernon"; "Botanical Garden Plant List"; and "The Vegetables, Herbs, and Fruits Grown at Mount Vernon."

7. Shoults, "The Home of the First Farmer," 604.

8. Ibid., 622–23; Johnson, *Mount Vernon*, 64.

9. Johnson, *Mount Vernon*, 64.

10. Blaine Harden, "First President's Childlessness Linked to Disease," *Washington Post*, February 29, 2004.

11. James Edward Peters, *Arlington National Cemetery: Shrine to America's Heroes* (Kensington, Md.: Woodbine House, 1986), 39, 283.

12. Ibid., 9–15.

13. Ibid., 18.

14. Ibid., 22.

15. Ibid., 22–23.

16. Ibid., 24–27.

17. Ibid., 24–26.

18. Ibid., 26–27.

19. Ibid., 36–37.

20. U.S. Congress, Senate, Committee on the District of Columbia, *Improvement of the Park System of the District of Columbia* (Washington: U.S. Government Printing Office, 1902), 58–59.

21. Nan Netherton and Ross Netherton, "Courthouses of Fairfax County," *Virginia Cavalcade*, Autumn 1977, 88.

22. Paul S. Dulaney, "The Architecture of Virginia County Courthouse Squares: A Neglected Heritage," *Newsletter, Institute of Government, University of Virginia* 43:11 (July 1967), 1.

23. Netherton and Netherton, "Courthouses," 90, 91. Wren's design with its portico and arches was later copied in the courthouses of Nelson (1807), Caroline (1808), Sussex (1825), and Madison (1829) counties. It remained popular in Virginia until preference shifted to Jefferson's classical design for the state capitol in 1825. (Nan Netherton and Ross Netherton, *Fairfax County in Virginia* [Norfolk, Va.: Donning, 1986].)

24. Netherton and Netherton, "Courthouses," 92.

25. Ibid., 95; Ross D. Netherton, letter to the author, October 29, 2005.

26. John G. Barnard, *A Report on the Defenses of Washington to the Chief of Engineers U.S. Army* (Washington: U.S. Government Printing Office, 1871), 18.

27. Ibid., 21.

28. Benjamin Franklin Cooling III and Walton H. Owen, Mr. Lincoln's Forts: *A Guide to the Civil War Defenses of Washington* (Shippensburg, Pa.: White Mane Publishing, 1988), 6.

29. Anne S. Frobel, *The Civil War Diary of Anne S. Frobel* (McLean, Va.: EPM Publications, 1992).

30. Cooling and Owen, *Mr. Lincoln's Forts*, 13.

31. Judith Beck Helm, *Tenleytown, DC, Country Village into City Neighborhood* (Washington: Tennally Press, 2000), 67–70; 199–200.

32. See http://alexandriava.gov/fortward.

5 *Robert Latou Dickinson (1861–1950)*

1. Raymond H. Torrey et al., *New York Walk Book* (New York: American Geographical Society, 1923).

2. George B. Barbour, "RLD, The Life of Robert Latou Dickinson, 1861–1950," manuscript, undated, 5–6, Robert Latou Dickinson Papers, Francis A. Countway Library of Medicine, Harvard Medical School, Boston, Mass. (hereinafter referred to as Dickinson Papers).

3. Ibid., 18.

4. Ibid., 25.

5. Ibid.

6. Ibid., 30.

7. Ibid.

8. Ibid., 49.

9. Ibid., 6.

10. Robert L. Dickinson, "Incidents in a Happy Life," manuscript, 11–12, Dickinson Papers.

11. Barbour, "RLD," 54.

12. Ibid., 53.

13. Ibid., 54–55.

14. James Reed, *The Birth Control Movement and American Society: From Private Vice to Public Virtue* (1978; reprint, Princeton University Press, 1984), 156.

15. Lura Beam, "The Doctor," manuscript, July 1, 1931, 2–10, Dickinson Papers.

16. Reed, *Birth Control Movement*, 165.

17. Ibid., 153.

18. Ibid., 161–62.

19. Ibid., 157.

20. Ibid., 153.

21. Ibid., 169.

22. Ibid., 182.

23. Ibid., 181, 184, 183.

24. Ibid., 186.

25. Gerard P. J. Griffin, "Robert Latou Dickinson, 21 February 1861– 29 November 1950," *Alumni Bulletin of the Long Island College of Medicine* 7:2 (April 1951), 6.

26. Reed, *Birth Control Movement*, 193.

27. Franklin H. Martin, *Digest of the Proceedings of the Council of National Defense during the World War* (Washington: U.S. Government Printing Office, 1934), 303.

28. Dickinson to Sarah T. Dickinson, Washington, DC, February 1918, Private family papers shared with the author.

29. Jean Marvin to Dorothy Barbour, Montclair, N.J., November 17, 1960, Dickinson Papers.

30. Dickinson to Sarah T. Dickinson, August 18, 1918, Private family papers.

31. Dickinson to Sarah T. Dickinson, August 25, 1918, Private family papers.

32. Conversations with mapmaker Eugene M. Scheel, Waterford, Va., and U.S. Geological Survey cartographers Peter De Vincentis and Scott Southworth, January to February 2004.

33. Dickinson to Sarah T. Dickinson, November 18, 1918, Private family papers.

34. Dickinson to Sarah T. Dickinson, late 1918, Private family papers.

35. See Malcolm L. Richardson, "An Index of Articles by the Rambler," 1996, Virginia Room, Fairfax Regional Library, Fairfax, Va.

36. Analysis of Dickinson's drawing materials by Terry D. Boone, Senior Rare Books Conservator, Library of Congress, January 9, 2004.

37. Barbour, "RLD," chap. 7.

38. Griffin, "Robert Latou Dickinson," 5.

39. Barbour, "RLD," chap. 7.

GEOLOGIC MAP OF THE POTOMAC RIVER GORGE

GREAT FALLS PARK, VIRGINIA, AND PART OF THE C&O CANAL NATIONAL HISTORIC PARK, MARYLAND

S. SCOTT SOUTHWORTH, CHIEF SCIENTIST
GIS AND COMPILATION BY DANIELLE DENENNY 2000

INTRODUCTION

This geologic map shows the types of rock and landforms of the Potomac River Gorge within the Piedmont physiographic province of the Central Appalachian region. The map was produced from information collected by geologists over a period of more than 25 years (Reed and Reed, 1969; Drake and Lee, 1989; Drake and Froelich, 1997; and Drake and others, 1999). The data were computerized to make a geographic information system (GIS) for the National Park Service and to provide a color map for park visitors. Readers are referred to The River and the Rocks (U.S. Geological Survey Bulletin 1471, by Reed and others, 1980) because it more fully describes the geology of the area.

Great Falls Park Locator Map

USGS 7.5-minute quadrangles

BEDROCK GEOLOGY

Most of the metamorphosed sedimentary rocks of the area are named the Mather Gorge Formation, after the rocks exposed there. They lack fossils but are interpreted to be about 600 millions years old. These rocks were originally deposited as sand, silt, and mud in an ancient sea, called the Iapetus Ocean, which existed before the Atlantic Ocean. Large blocks and fragments eroded from an older igneous rock (map unit CZu) were mixed with the sediments. Igneous rocks--hot, molten rocks deep below the Earth's surface-were injected up into the sedimentary rocks at various times in the geologic past. These igneous rocks, and their times of emplacement, include amphibolite (about 540 million years ago), granodiorite and pegmatite (about 470 million years ago), and lamprophyre (about 360 million years ago).

The sedimentary rocks were changed by heat and pressure (metamorphosed) and deformed during several collisions of the Earth's continental plates that resulted in the formation of the Appalachian Mountains. Metamorphism changed the sedimentary and igneous rocks into schist and gneiss (map unit CZms), and migmatite (map unit CZmm). Hot solutions of silica were injected as veins of white quartz into the rocks, and crystals of muscovite (white mica), biotite (black mica), garnet, staurolite, and kyanite grew as the rocks cooled. Some of the vein quartz nearby in Maryland was extensively prospected and mined for gold from 1861 to 1951; note the abandoned prospect sites on the map. The metamorphosed rocks are tightly folded, they are well layered with mica-rich foliation planes, and locally they contain close-spaced fractures.

LANDSCAPE EVOLUTION

The landscape of the area is mostly the result of erosion by the Potomac River during the past 5 million years. As the Potomac River flows to the southeast, it cuts obliquely across several types of north-trending bedrock units. The river follows the trend of joints (cracks) and faults along the straight river course in Mather Gorge.

Level surfaces called terraces, which have been cut into bedrock at different elevations by the Potomac River, form conspicuous features of the landscape. The terraces are actually remnants of old flood plains of the downcutting Potomac. There are at least six recognizable terrace levels, but they are all shown combined in order to be more readable at the map scale. The highest and oldest terrace is on the crest of Glade Hill in Great Falls Park, where a deposit of river boulders of quartzite and diabase is found (unit QTb).

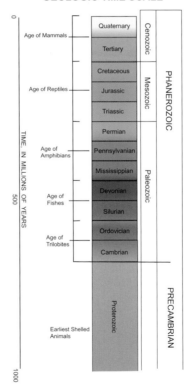

GEOLOGIC TIME SCALE

The Great Falls Park entrance, parking lots, picnic area, visitor center, and Patowmack Canal are on the second highest and next oldest terrace. When the Potomac River was downcutting through this terrace into the bedrock, Glade Hill was an island. There are at least four younger terrace levels within the gorge. Downcutting by the Potomac River into these terraces has created islands, islets, pinnacles, shoestring channels, oxbows, plungepools, and potholes. The erosional features are best seen on Bear Island. The C&O Canal utilizes an abandoned channel of the Potomac River at Widewater that in part creates Bear Island. Alluvial stream deposits are best preserved along parts of Difficult Run, whereas most alluvial deposits along the Potomac River have been removed during floods. The bedrock terraces provide excellent exposures of Piedmont bedrock and the fascinating landforms eroded into them.

DESCRIPTION OF MAP UNITS

SURFICIAL DEPOSITS

Qaf — Artificial fill and ground disturbed by construction

Qal — Alluvium (Holocene—present to 10,000 years old)—Unconsolidated clay, silt, sand, gravel, and cobbles in valley bottoms

Qg — Alluvial gravel-bar deposits along Difficult Run (Holocene and late Pleistocene—present to 100,000 years old)

Qcd — Colluvium (Holocene and late Pleistocene—present to 100,000 years old)—Cobbles, boulders, and debris in slope hollows

QTa — Unconsolidated clay, silt, sand, and gravel deposited on level surfaces called terraces (Holocene and Pliocene—10,000 to 5 million years old)

QTb — Boulder deposit on crest of Glade Hill; is remnant of highest and oldest terrace (Holocene and Pliocene—10,000 to 5 million years old)

OLDER IGNEOUS ROCKS

Dl — Lamprophyre dikes (Late Devonian-about 360 million years old)—Dark-colored, biotite mica-rich tabular intrusions that cut across the surrounding rock

Ob — Bear Island Granodiorite and pegmatite bodies (Ordovician-about 470 million years old)—Light-colored, muscovite mica-rich, elliptical intrusive bodies and small tabular intrusions

Ca — Amphibolite sills (Early Cambrian-about 540 million years old)—Dark-colored, hornblende-rich tabular intrusions, emplaced parallel to the bedding of the surrounding rock

METAMORPHOSED SEDIMENTARY ROCKS
(Lower Cambrian and (or) Late Proterozoic—about 600 million years old)
Sykesville Formation

CZs — Melange—Gray, fine-grained mixture of quartz and feldspar, with pebbles of white quartz and blocks of greenish-gray phyllonite; originally deposited on the ocean floor

Mather Gorge Formation

CZms — Quartz-rich schist and mica gneiss—Greenish-gray rocks with different textures; schist is finer grained, more planar, and less massive than gneiss

CZmg — Metagraywacke and metasiltstone schist—Well-bedded, gray, dirty sandstone interbedded with siltstone; originally deposited in submarine turbidity currents on the ocean floor

CZmm — Migmatite—Complex, light- and dark-gray rock formed when rocks of different ages were melted together

CZmp — Phyllonite with vein quartz—Shiny, greenish-gray, fine-grained sheared rock with pods and veins of white quartz

OLDER IGNEOUS ROCKS

CZu — Ultramafic rocks—Dark-green igneous rocks consisting of serpentinite, soapstone, and talc schist; occur as sedimentary blocks and fragments in the Mather Gorge Formation

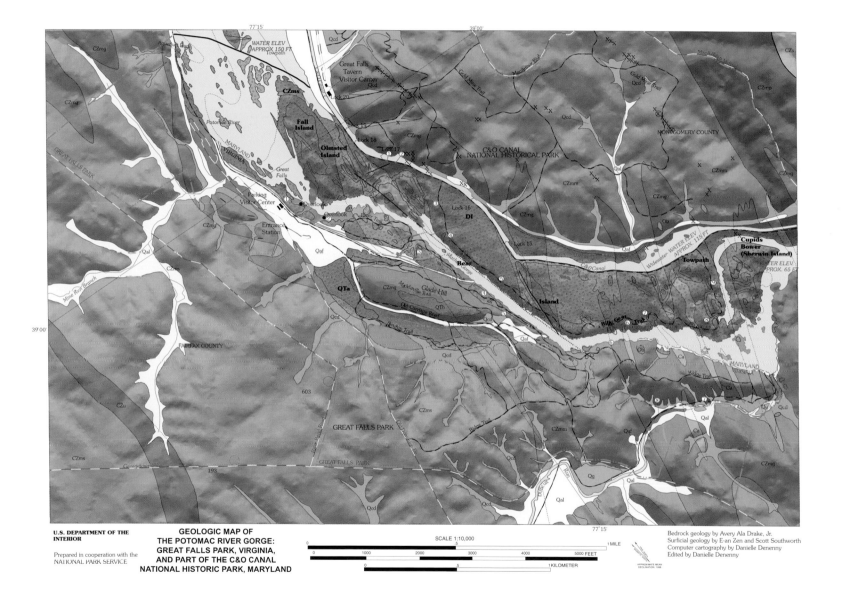

GEOLOGIC MAP OF
THE POTOMAC RIVER GORGE:
GREAT FALLS PARK, VIRGINIA,
AND PART OF THE C&O CANAL
NATIONAL HISTORIC PARK, MARYLAND

U.S. DEPARTMENT OF THE
INTERIOR

Prepared in cooperation with the
NATIONAL PARK SERVICE

Bedrock geology by Avery Ala Drake, Jr.
Surficial geology by E-an Zen and Scott Southworth
Computer cartography by Danielle Denenny
Edited by Danielle Denenny

SCALE 1:10,000

1 MILE

5000 FEET

1 KILOMETER

APPROXIMATE MEAN
DECLINATION: 1998

SELECT BIBLIOGRAPHY

Achenbach, Joel. "Potomac Dreaming." *Washington Post Magazine,*
May 5, 2002.

The Adams Memorial. Pamphlet. Washington: Rock Creek Cemetery, 1997.

Armed Forces Retirement Home. "Historic Buildings at the U.S. Soldiers' and
Airmen's Home." Photocopied handout, undated.

Armstrong, Edith Martin. "A Brief History of Cabin John Park." Manuscript,
1947. Montgomery County Historical Society vertical files.

Atwood, Albert. "Potomac River Destiny." *National Geographic Magazine,*
July 1945.

Audubon Society of the District of Columbia. *The Potomac Valley:
History and Prospect.* Washington: Audubon Society of the District of
Columbia, 1952.

Barbour, George B. "The Life of Robert Latou Dickinson, 1861–1950." Undated
manuscript. Robert Latou Dickinson Papers. Francis A. Countway Library of
Medicine, Harvard University.

Barnard, John G. *A Report on the Defenses of Washington to the Chief of
Engineers,* U.S. Army. Washington: U.S. Government Printing Office, 1871.

Beddow, Reid. "Cabin John." *Washington Post,* December 8, 1963.

Bishop, Joseph B. *Theodore Roosevelt's Letters to His Children.* New York: New
American Library of World Literature, 1964.

Brookhiser, Richard. *Founding Father: Rediscovering George Washington.* New
York: Free Press, 1996.

Buerger, Christian, and Ramin Javedan. "The Trolley to Great Falls."
Essay Awards, Historical Society of Fairfax County, Virginia, vol. 2, 1988.

Church, Joanna. "A Bridge to Cabin John's History." *Gazette,* July 24, 1998.

Cook, Eleonor M. V. "A History of Early Water Mills in Montgomery County,
Maryland." Manuscript, 1990. Montgomery County Historical Society,
Rockville, Md.

Cook, Richard, and Deborah Lange. *Glen Echo Park: A Story of Survival.* Glen Echo, Md.: Bethesda Communications Group, 2000.

Cooke, Elizabeth Miles. *The History of the Georgetown Pike.* Annandale, Va.: Elizabeth Miles Cooke and Charles Baptie Studios, 1977.

Cooling, Benjamin Franklin III, and Walton H. Owen. *Mr. Lincoln's Forts: A Guide to the Civil War Defenses of Washington.* Shippensburg, Pa.: White Mane Publishing, 1988.

Council of National Defense. *Second Annual Report of the Council of National Defense for the Fiscal Year Ended June 30, 1918.* Washington, 1918.

Curtis, William T. S. "Cabin John Bridge." *Records of the Columbia Historical Society,* 1897.

Davis, Harriet Riddle. "Civil War Recollections of a Little Yankee." *Records of the Columbia Historical Society,* 1944.

Dickinson, Robert L. "Incidents in a Happy Life." Typescript of recorded family conversation, December 1950, 11–12. Robert Latou Dickinson Papers, Francis A. Countway Library of Medicine, Harvard University, Boston, Mass.

Downing, Margaret Brent. "The Centenary of Clara Barton and Recent Biographical Sketches of Her Life and Achievements." *Records of the Columbia Historical Society,* 1922.

Dulaney, Paul S. "The Architecture of Virginia County Courthouse Squares: A Neglected Heritage." *Newsletter, Institute of Government, University of Virginia* 43:11 (July 1967).

Fearson, Jim. "Chain Bridge: A History of the Bridge and Its Surrounding Territory, 1608–1991." *Arlington Historical Magazine* 9 (October 1991): 8–9.

"The Fiftieth Anniversary of the U.S. Department of Justice Building." Manuscript, 1984. U.S. Department of Justice Library.

Fradin, Morris. *Hey-Ey-Ey, Lock! Adventure on the Chesapeake and Ohio Canal.* Cabin John, Md.: See and Know Press, 1974.

Frobel, Anne S. *The Civil War Diary of Anne S. Frobel.* McLean, Va.: EPM Publications, 1992.

Gaillard, D. D. "The Washington Aqueduct and Cabin John Bridge." *National Geographic Magazine*, December 1897.

Garrett, Wendell, ed. *George Washington's Mount Vernon*. New York: Montacelli Press, 1998.

Garrett, Wilbur E. "The Patowmack Canal: Waterway That Led to the Constitution. *National Geographic Magazine* 171: 6 (June 1987).

Goode, Paul R. *The United States Soldiers' Home*. Richmond, Va.: William Byrd Press, 1957.

Green, Constance McLaughlin. *The Church on Lafayette Square, 1815–1970*. Washington: Potomac Books, 1970.

Greenberg, Allan. *George Washington, Architect*. New York: Andreas Papadakis, 1999.

Griswold, Mac. *Washington's Gardens at Mount Vernon*. Boston: Houghton, Mifflin Company, 1999.

Grosvenor, Gilbert. "The Great Falls of the Potomac." *National Geographic Magazine*, March 1928.

Hagner, Alexander. "History and Reminiscences of St. John's Church, Washington, DC." *Records of the Columbia Historical Society*, 1908.

Hahn, Thomas F. "Swiftwater." *Chesapeake and Ohio Canal: Old Picture Album*. Shepherdstown, W. Va.: The American Canal and Transportation Center, 1979.

_____ . *Towpath Guide to the C&O Canal*. Shepherdstown, W. Va.: American Canal and Transportation Center, 1982. Reprint 1990.

Halle, Louis J. *Spring in Washington*. New York: William Sloane Association, 1947.

Harden, Blaine. "First President's Childlessness Linked to Disease." *Washington Post*, February 29, 2004.

Helm, Judith Beck. *Tenleytown, D.C., Country Village into City Neighborhood*. Washington: Tennally Press, 2000.

Heritage Cavaliers. *The Nation's Capital*. Washington: Heritage Cavaliers, 1967.

High, Mike. *The C&O Canal Companion*. Baltimore, Md.: Johns Hopkins University Press, 2000.

Hildebrand, J. R. "The Sources of Washington's Charm." *National Geographic Magazine*, June 1923.

Historic American Buildings Survey/Historic American Engineering Record. HABS no. DC-673. Prints and Photographs Division, Library of Congress.

Isberg, Emily. "Cabin John: Blue Collar Town Attracts Artists, Professionals." *Sentinel*, August 1, 1979.

Johnson, Gerald W. *Mount Vernon: The Story of a Shrine*. Epilogue by Ellen McCallister. Mount Vernon: The Mount Vernon Ladies' Association, 2002.

Keim, D. Randolph. *Keim's Illustrated Handbook: Washington and Its Environs*. Washington: privately published, 1874.

King, Leroy O., Jr. *100 Years of Capital Traction*. College Park, Md.: Taylor Publishing Co., 1972.

Kurian, George Thomas, ed. *A Historical Guide to the U.S. Government*. New York: Oxford University Press, 1998.

Kytle, Elizabeth. *Time Was: A Cabin John Memory Book*. Cabin John, Md.: Cabin John Citizens' Association, 1976.

Leech, Margaret. *Reveille in Washington, 1860–1865*. New York: Harper and Brothers, 1941.

Leupp, Francis E. *Walks about Washington*. Drawings by Lester G. Hornby. Boston: Little Brown, 1915.

Mackintosh, Barry. *C&O Canal: The Making of a Park*. Washington: U.S. Department of the Interior, National Park Service, 1991.

Marriott, J. H. Wilson. "Picturesque Cabin John, a Bit of History." Manuscript, 1903. Vertical files, Montgomery County Historical Society.

Martin, Franklin H. *Digest of the Proceedings of the Council of National Defense during the World War*. Washington: U.S. Government Printing Office, 1934.

Myer, Donald B. *Bridges and the City of Washington*. Washington: U.S. Commission of Fine Arts, 1974.

_____ . "Cabin John Bridge, a Washington Landmark." Manuscript, 1973. Vertical files, Montgomery County Historical Society.

National Archives. Council of National Defense, Preliminary Inventory no. 2, RG 62. Washington, DC, December 1942. National Archives and Records Administration, Washington, DC.

Netherton, Nan, and Ross Netherton. "Courthouses of Fairfax County." *Virginia Cavalcade*, Autumn 1977, 88.

_____ . *Fairfax County in Virginia*. Norfolk: Donning, 1986.

Netherton, Ross D., and Ruby Waldeck. *The Fairfax Courthouse*. Fairfax, Va.: Fairfax County Office of Comprehensive Planning, 1977.

Olszewski, George. *Franklin Park*. Washington, DC: Division of History, Office of Archaeology and Historic Preservation, 1970.

Peters, James Edward. *Arlington National Cemetery: Shrine to America's Heroes*. Kensington, Md.: Woodbine House, 1986.

Pinsker, Matthew. *Lincoln's Sanctuary: Abraham Lincoln and the Soldiers' Home*. New York: Oxford University Press, 2003.

"Potomac Almanac, History of Potomac." Manuscript, 1970. C&O Canal Library, Hagerstown, Md.

Powell, Helen. "Helen Powell, in Her Own Words." *Prince George's Exeter*, January 27, 1999.

Reed, James. *The Birth Control Movement and American Society: From Private Vice to Public Virtue*. New York: Basic Books, 1978. Reprint, Princeton: Princeton University Press, 1984.

"The Run Looking from John's Cabin." *Evening Star*, April 6, 1913.

Russell, Paul. "Japanese Spring in America." *Asia* 30 (May 1930).

Sanderlin, Walter S. *A Study of the History of the Potomac River Valley*. Report. Chap. 8. Washington: U.S. Department of the Interior, National Park Service, [undated; ca. 1940s].

Schafer, Edith. *Aspects of Georgetown*. Washington: Flaneur Press, 2004.

Shannon, J. Harry. ["The Rambler," pseud.] Collected *Evening Star* columns on microfiche, Fairfax County Public Library.

Shosteck, Robert. *Guide to Trails around Washington.* New York: Rotolith, 1937.

Shoults, Worth E. "The Home of the First Farmer of America." *National Geographic Magazine,* May 1928.

Skramstad, Harold K. "The Engineer as Architect in Washington: The Contribution of Montgomery Meigs." *Records of the Columbia Historical Society,* 1969–1970.

Smith, Kathryn Schneider, ed. *Washington at Home: An Illustrated History of Neighborhoods in the Nation's Capital.* Eugene, Ore.: Windsor Publications, 1988.

Souvenir History of Cabin John Bridge. Washington: W. H. Brewton, n.d.

Spilsbury, Gail. *Rock Creek Park.* Baltimore, Md.: Johns Hopkins University Press, 2002.

Spratt, Jack. "Rock Creek's Bridges." *Records of the Columbia Historical Society,* 1953–1956.

Stanton, Richard L. *Potomac Journey: Fairfax Stone to Tidewater.* Washington: Smithsonian Institution, 1993.

Sween, Jane C., and William Offutt. *Montgomery County, Centuries of Change.* Sun Valley, Calif.: American Historical Press, 1999.

Theroux, Phyllis. "Cabin John." *Washington Post,* June 5, 1977.

Tilp, Frederick. *This Was Potomac River.* Alexandria, Va.: Frederick Tilp, 1978.

Torrey, Raymond H., Frank Place Jr., and Robert L. Dickinson. *New York Walk Book.* New York: American Geographical Society, 1923.

Two Hundred Twenty-Fifth Anniversary, St. Paul's Episcopal Church. Booklet. Washington: Rock Creek Parish, 1944.

U.S. Congress, Senate, Committee on the District of Columbia. *Improvement of the Park System of the District of Columbia.* Washington: U.S. Government Printing Office, 1902.

U.S. Department of the Interior, National Park Service. *Clara Barton.* Washington: U.S. Department of the Interior, 1981.

U.S. Department of Justice. Brochure. Washington: U.S. Department of Justice, 1998.

U.S. Department of Justice. Federal Bureau of Investigation. "Principal Offices of the FBI—Past and Present." Undated manuscript page in the FBI historian's office.

Wagner, Arlo. "Cabin John Out of Step with Rest of Montgomery County." *Washington Times*, March 6, 1989.

Ways, Harry C. "The Washington Aqueduct, 1852–1992." [Washington?]: H. C. Ways, [1996?].

Wilson, Guy, ed. *Buildings of Virginia, Tidewater and Piedmont.* New York: Oxford University Press, 2002.

Writers' Program of the Work Projects Administration in the State of Virginia. *Virginia: A Guide to the Old Dominion.* American Guide Series. New York: Oxford University Press, 1940.

Young, Joanne, and Taylor Biggs Lewis Jr. *Washington's Mount Vernon.* New York: Holt, Rinehart and Winston, 1973.

Yowell, J. "The Cabin of John." Undated brochure. Historical Society of Washington, DC.